John Taverner

his Life and Music

Colin Hand

EULENBURG BOOKS
LONDON

Ernst Eulenburg Ltd
48 Great Marlborough Street
London W1V 2BN

Copyright © 1978, Colin Hand

First published in 1978 by Ernst Eulenburg Ltd

ISBN 0 903873 51 6 (cased)
        0 903873 52 4 (paperback)

Printed and bound in England by
Caligraving Ltd, Thetford, Norfolk

CONTENTS

An illustration of John Taverner (see p. 35) from the Forrest-Heyther part-books, reproduced by kind permission of the Bodleian Library, Oxford

INTRODUCTION

For many years John Taverner has remained one of the most enigmatic figures in English music. There has never been a lack of reference to him either in modern encyclopaedias or histories of music, but the sequence of events that has for long constituted an outline of the composer's life is, to say the least, singular. Although accounts vary in detail from one author to another, the basic pattern is the same, beginning with his birth in or near Tattershall in South Lincolnshire about 1495. Some writers credit him with having spent a few years in London during his early manhood, basing their claim upon an entry in a City Gild Register of 1514. He next appears in 1525 as a member of the staff at the Collegiate Church at Tattershall, which he left in 1526 to become choirmaster at Cardinal Wolsey's newly founded College at Oxford. The following year we read of his becoming involved with the Lutheran heretics there, of his conversion to Protestantism, and of being party to concealing anti-papal literature beneath the floorboards of his school. He was therefore thrown into prison, but subsequently released by Wolsey on the grounds of being 'but a musician'.[1] Two years after this incident he left Oxford, and, 'under pressure of religious conviction',[2] abandoned musical composition altogether. He then spent the remainder of his career acting as an agent for Thomas Cromwell in the suppression of monastic foundations. In 1537 we find him engaged in 'fanatical persecution'[3] in Boston, with the public burning of the Rood in the market place offered as evidence of his change of heart. The same year we read of his election to the Gild of Corpus Christi, a Catholic-based community in Boston, and in the last year of his life of his appointment as one of the first aldermen of the newly-created Borough. He died in October, 1545, and, according to his

1 John Foxe, *Acts and Monuments*, 1563 edition.
2 E. H. Fellowes, *Grove's Dictionary of Music and Musicians*, (1954) Vol. VIII, p. 323.
3 *Ibid.*

widow's will, was buried under the bell-tower of Boston Parish Church.

Clearly this picture does little for Taverner's reputation and nothing to endear him to the faith for which he wrote most of his music. More important, however, it raises questions as to its degree of accuracy since certain features of the outline just given are hardly acceptable on the grounds of commonsense alone. Why, for example, did Taverner continue in office for another two years after the Oxford heresy incident and his supposed conversion to Protestantism? How could he possibly accept election to a Catholic Gild in Boston in 1537 when he was simultaneously engaged in the persecution of the Roman Church? And how, in reference to his output, does one explain his extended stylistic development and the use of techniques that rightly belong to the mid-sixteenth century, in a person whose creative career was supposedly abandoned in 1530? In short, we must ask how such a biographical account as that outlined above originated, and upon what evidence it was based.

In order to answer this question it is necessary to look back to the earliest literary references to Taverner, namely those by the sixteenth-century Protestant martyrologist, John Foxe, writing in his *Acts and Monuments* of 1563. It is here that we first find an account of the Oxford heresy incident, whose details the author learnt from a certain Anthony Dalaber, a scholar who had been involved in the affair. Included in the account is a description of Taverner's part in the conspiracy — that of hiding books beneath the floorboards of his school — and his escaping imprisonment through the intervention of Wolsey. Then follows the well-known and oft-quoted marginal note, 'This Taverner repented him very much that he had made songs to popish ditties in the time of his blindness'.

No statement could have caused more confusion and misunderstanding. Despite the fact that it was simply a personal comment by Foxe in a work that is coloured by his own religious affiliations, the quotation was seized upon by early historians in whose hands it became the central feature of all Taverner biographies, and was accepted as evidence of the composer's rejection of the Roman faith. The fact that he continued to serve Wolsey's Chapel for two years after the incident appears to have been overlooked.

The first historians to use Foxe's account were Thomas Fuller writing in his *Church History of Britain* in 1655, and Anthony à Wood in *Athenae Oxoniensis* compiled some thirty years later. In

8

the following century John Hawkins in his *General History of the Science and Practice of Music* (1776) could only repeat Fuller's account, and even Charles Burney in his *General History of Music* completed in 1789 could throw no further light upon the subject. It was not until the resurgence of interest in Tudor church music during the early years of this century that we find any other accounts relating to Taverner's life and work. In 1920 W. H. Grattan Flood produced a biographical outline of the composer which he claimed was based upon documentary evidence and 'other first-hand sources'. The origins of this newly-acquired information, however, were not named, so that when the editors came to write the preface to the publication of Taverner's Masses in 1923 they were thrown back upon the original accounts already quoted. Furthermore, when E. H. Fellowes produced his biographical survey of the composer for the third edition of Grove's *Dictionary of Music and Musicians*, he found it unnecessary to question the validity of Foxe's famous marginal note.

One of the major problems in Taverner research is the dearth of reliable documented information about the composer's life. Equally problematic is the sifting of those biographical accounts that have already been written, and the rejection of those passages that have been based upon comment rather than fact, and that have proved so misleading. When this sifting has been done, however, (an essential course of action if we are to try to build up a fair and accurate picture of the composer), we shall find that the only relevant documentary evidence available to us today is that covering two periods of his life. The first extends from 1525 to 1530 during which time he was initially at the Collegiate Church at Tattershall and later at Cardinal College, Oxford, and the second from 1537 until his death in 1545 when he was active in various capacities in Boston. To supplement these records, two other important sources of information have survived, namely the *Inquisition post mortem* on the composer's property, and his wife's will. Beyond this we can only rely upon contemporary accounts, the manuscripts of his works, and a critical examination of his musical style in an attempt to fill some of the existing gaps which at present include his date and place of birth, his education, especially his musical training, his early years of manhood, and a problematic period from 1530 to 1537.

Although the biographical picture is still far from complete, we have fared better with the music, even though some of the manuscripts are now in an advanced state of deterioration, caused partly by ink corrosion. A number of references to Taverner's compositions appear in treatises by early historians, and both Hawkins and Burney quote actual passages from his music. The most important contribution however was the publication in 1923-4 of his complete extant works in Volumes I and III of the Tudor Church Music Series edited by P. C. Buck, E. H. Fellowes, A. Ramsbotham, R. R. Terry, and S. T. Warner. The preparation of the series was an outstanding piece of scholarship, and the editing of the music was carried out with the greatest care for detail, even to the extent of noting any variations in a work that occurred in more than one manuscript. After being out of print for several years, the series has now been re-issued in smaller format by Edwin F. Kalmus of New York, and is available in this country from Universal Edition.

Boston, May 1977   C. H.

PART I

HIS LIFE

The first reference to John Taverner the musician is contained in a document recording a visit to Tattershall College by the Chancellor to the Bishop of Lincoln on 15 May 1525. The document[1], now preserved in the Lincolnshire Archives, lists the composer among six *clerici socii* or clerk-fellows of the College. There is no indication of his age at the time or of how long he had been at Tattershall, and the list does not show him as holding any position of responsibility in the establishment.

The College was a thriving community in Tudor times, and the manorial complex of which it was a part was the culmination of years of vision and effort on the part of its owners and patrons. The original plans for such a complex consisting of a castle, a church, a college, a school and dwellings including almshouses were initiated by Ralph, third Lord Cromwell (1403-55). He had inherited from his grandfather the nearby manor and lands of Tattershall Thorpe, which had been acquired by the first Lord Cromwell through his marriage to a descendant of the Eudo Fitzspirewic family whose ownership of them is recorded in Domesday Book.

Cromwell's ambitious scheme was put into operation in 1433, but he only lived to see the completion in 1455 of the first phase of the project, the castle whose impressive brick tower still stands as a landmark in the flat countryside of South Lincolnshire. Nevertheless, plans relating to other features of the manorial community were implemented during Cromwell's lifetime, including the granting of a licence in 1439 to rebuild the parish church, converting it into a college of seven chaplains, one of whom was to be Master or Warden, six lay-clerks and six choristers. The following year (1440) the charter was signed establishing the college, and its first members were named. These together with the Master were housed in temporary accommodation until the building was completed. 'Statutes and Ordinances for the College

1 *Visitations in the Diocese of Lincoln*, iii pp. 111-113, ref. L. f. 9.

11

and Almshouse of the Holy Trinity at Tattershall' issued after Cromwell's death, along with articles pertaining to the foundation of the College, provide us with fairly detailed information about the duties of the collegiate community, together with the remuneration received by each member. One regulation stated that the Master and chaplains must be in residence at Tattershall for at least forty-eight weeks each year, whilst clerks were appointed on a less regular basis. The chaplains' duties were mainly liturgical, though they would no doubt be competent in singing plainsong. The musical responsibilities would fall mainly on the shoulders of the clerks and choristers who would be capable of singing works of a polyphonic nature. Provision was made in the 'Statutes and Ordinances' for the hiring of four men 'skilled in song and reading' and four boys' 'teachable in song and reading' to help the resident clerks and choristers on festal occasions or when some were on leave. (Both chaplains and clerks were allowed four weeks' holiday each year.)

Even at this early stage, Cromwell's establishment at Tattershall had become a place of some importance, as the emoluments received by its resident staff clearly show. The yearly salary of the Master was twenty pounds, that of the chaplains ten pounds, and the clerks were paid nearly eight pounds per annum. In addition, extra payments were made to chaplains and clerks for organ-playing and for providing singing tuition for choristers.

Although Tattershall was not a monastic foundation, the duties of the staff were comparable with one, and the Offices as well as the Mass were celebrated daily and strictly in accordance with the statutes of the College. The Canonical Hours of Prime, Terce, Sext and None were attended by at least four chaplains or clerks. The choristers sang Matins at 7 am, followed by the celebration of Mass sung polyphonically with organ, and completed the day with Vespers and Compline at 3.30 pm. Low Mass was said daily by the chaplains, and the Litany was sung on three days each week. In addition, feast days were appropriately marked, and special prayers and masses were said for the king and for the soul of Lord Cromwell. From this we may safely deduce that, by the middle of the fifteenth century, the collegiate community had built up a considerable reputation both liturgically and musically, the latter borne out by the care that was placed upon the hiring of extra clerks and choristers.

The death of Cromwell in 1455 must have given the College brethren some cause for concern. Having no children, his title passed to a nephew who was later killed at the Battle of Barnet in 1471. This nephew appears to have done little or nothing towards the building of the College, and at his death the manor became Crown property. Meanwhile the community had lost not only their founder, but their Warden, William More, who died in 1456, followed two years later by the castle architect. By good fortune, however, Warden More was succeeded in 1458 by a certain John Gigur, a fellow of Merton College, Oxford, who quickly proved himself a most able administrator. He took upon himself the task of completing the building project as well as maintaining divine service according to the statutes of the College. By further good fortune, William Waynflete, Bishop of Winchester and friend of the late Lord Cromwell, became patron of the foundation at Tattershall. He was able to pour the necessary financial resources into the project so that, at his death in 1486, Cromwell's dream had become reality, and the entire complex, including the college, the grammar school, the almshouse and the magnificent perpendicular-style church, was virtually complete.

On the death of Bishop Waynflete, the manor was given by the King, Henry VII, to his mother, Margaret Beaufort. No better patron could have been found. She was a champion of learning, and anxious to maintain the standards of education and ritual that had become an integral part of the collegiate establishment. Gigur remained as Master until his resignation in 1502 when he was succeeded by a Lincolnshire man, Henry Horneby, Chancellor and Dean of Margaret Beaufort's Chapel. Except for a four-year period from 1509 to 1513, he held the post of Warden until his death in 1518, by which time the manor had become Crown property.

With the building scheme complete and the full complement of chaplains, clerks and choristers now in residence under their Warden, John Custable (in office from 1518 to 1528), we arrive at the point at which the name of John Taverner first appears as a member of the fraternity. The document which lists the composer's name together with five other clerk-fellows and six chaplains is a record made by the Chancellor, John Rayne, of his visit to Tattershall College on the instructions of John Longland, Bishop of Lincoln. According to his record, several residents made personal comments on the work and conditions at the College, but Taverner's contribution gives no more information beyond the fact that one of the chaplain's rooms was in need of repair.

According to W. H. Grattan Flood, writing in 1925,[2] Taverner

2 *Early Tudor Composers*, p. 49.

was Master of the Choristers at the time of the Chancellor's visitation, and was also by then a 'composer of fame'. As was his wont, the author gives no indication of the source of these observations, and the Tattershall records throw no light on the subject. All the same, these statements, which cannot be totally ignored, do raise the whole question of Taverner's whereabouts prior to 1525.

His birthplace is still unknown; we know nothing about his parents, and only the sketchiest of information relating to his family can as yet be found. Most biographers, however, suggest that he was born in the vicinity of Tattershall, and his associations with the College add some weight to this supposition, along with the fact that his colleagues there in 1525 were all local men. In his *Acts and Monuments*[3] John Foxe describes Taverner as 'of Boston', but whilst we know that he spent at least the last eight years of his life in the town, there is too little evidence for regarding it as his birthplace. There is also insufficient evidence to support the theory that he might have been a chorister at Tattershall, although there is no doubt that, had he been born in or near the place, any musical promise he might have shown as a boy would most certainly have been given a chance to develop in the thriving community already described. The College accounts make numerous collective references to choristers including one in the 1492-3 entry, recording payment for 'fitting, sewing and making ten cloaks' for the boys, a clear indication that the choir by this time had reached its full complement; but in only one instance do the accounts mention any chorister by name.

We are in no way helped by the fact that Taverner was a relatively common name in Tudor times. Derivation alone would suggest its frequent occurrence, and this is substantiated by genealogical publications which list several families of that name in Lincolnshire and its neighbouring counties, as well as in other parts of the country. According to the *Inquisition post mortem* on John Taverner's property,[4] which was drawn up in 1546, a certain William Taverner is named as brother and 'next heir' to the composer. At the time this William was *xl annos et amplius* — forty years of age and more. Another document now preserved in the Lincoln Archives Office[5] and dated 1557 is the will also of a William Taverner, a farmer whose home was at Tattershall. It is quite possible that he and the composer's brother were one and

3   1563 edition, p. 497.
4   London Public Record Office, MS.C. 142/74/130.
5   Consistory Court Wills, III f. 28.

the same person, though this has been disputed on the grounds that no mention is made in the will of any lands inherited from John Taverner. It is also possible that a Thomas Taverner, an innkeeper at Billingborough, a village midway between Boston and Grantham, was related to the composer for in *his* will[6] he makes a bequest to the Tattershall farmer's son, John. This would suggest his kinship with William and hence with the composer, but any further attempt to link the families would at present only add to the confusion that already exists.

Another problem has to do with Taverner's date of birth. We have no reference to his age at any point in his career; the *Inquisition post mortem* records only the date on which he died, and so far his will has not been traced. For many years, 1495 has been quoted by music historians as the year in which he was born, and this might yet prove to be correct. In the introduction to his works in the Tudor Church Music Series, the editors suggest some time between 1495 and 1500 as being most acceptable, basing their argument upon his appointment to Cardinal College, Oxford in 1526. It is unlikely, they claim, that he was less than twenty-five years old at the time, as he must have already achieved a considerable musical reputation before being invited to take up so important a post as that at Wolsey's new foundation. This is feasible, even if unsubstantiated, but it does not take into account a possible sojourn in London during the second decade of the sixteenth century, a point upon which scholars are still divided. The disagreement hinges upon an entry in the Bede Roll or register[7] of the Fraternity of St Nicholas, the London Gild of Parish Clerks. Included in its list of new members in 1514 is a certain John Taverner and his wife, Annes. There is admittedly no proof that this man and the composer were one and the same person, though there is a strong and convincing case for linking the two. Several other John Taverners are recorded as living in London at the time of the Bede Roll entry, but information about them, together with details of their trades and activities, points conclusively to their having no connections with either the St Nicholas Gild member or the clerk-fellow of Tattershall. If the London Gild Taverner were the composer, the earliest date of birth suggested by the Tudor Church Music Editors, namely 1495, would mean that he was only nineteen when he joined the Fraternity. This is very unlikely since members of similar and kindred gilds served a seven-year apprenticeship before receiving the

6 Consistory Court Wills, f. 150.
7 Guildhall Library, London, MS. 4889.

freedom of the City at twenty-four years of age. A date around 1490 as suggested by some scholars[8] would therefore be more realistic.

The Gild of St Nicholas was founded probably as far back as the thirteenth century as a charitable concern, and was granted a new charter in 1449 from which time records have been preserved. Parish clerks' duties were mainly musical, though they did include the keeping of church records. Apart from participating in the regular services of their church, they attended civic functions, sang Mass after the election of a Lord Mayor, and assisted in services of dedication. They celebrated musically the induction of new members to the Gild, and sang at the funeral services of deceased brethren. In entirely different fields (though less markedly separated in mediaeval times than in later centuries), they performed miracle plays and secular pageants on feast days. Their varied activities provided regular work for the many free-lance musicians in London at the time, and parish clerks would often hire the services of other clerks and conducts or laymen to assist them on special occasions. Membership of the Fraternity of St Nicholas was compulsory for all parish clerks and conducts within the City and surrounding districts, and the rules of the Gild were rigorously applied, with heavy fines imposed on erring brothers.

In addition to its role outlined above, the Fraternity had within its bounds a membership that extended far beyond its descriptive title, and included monarchy, high ranking churchmen, and civic dignitaries as well as the clerks, laymen and their wives. In short, it functioned as a club for the study and performance of music, as well as satisfying the requirements of the church. In company with such distinguished names as Lady Margaret Beaufort, Bishop Alcock, Chancellor of England, and William Caxton, its membership embraced a large number of well-known composers of the day including Thomas Appulby, John Cook, William Cornyshe, Robert Fayrfax, Nicholas Ludford, Henry Prentys and John Sheppard. The presence of a John Taverner in this list points to the same person who was to feature later in Tattershall, Oxford and Boston.

Before placing too much emphasis upon this possible connection, however, we must first consider what advantages London might offer a young aspiring musician, and second, try to ascertain whether or not there is evidence beyond the Bede Roll entry

8 Including Denis Stevens in an article on John Taverner in *Die Musik in Geschichte und Gegenwart.*

to suggest that Taverner did spend some time in the City.

In Tudor times, London was the foremost centre of musical activity in England, enjoying the support and patronage of royalty, nobility and leaders of the church. Henry VIII's own interests extended far beyond his ability in composition and instrumental practice. He contributed in no small measure to the development of music in this country by encouraging the visits of foreign composers, by building up a valuable collection of instruments and manuscripts, and by commissioning new works for performance by his personal musicians, which included the Chapel Royal and the King's Musick. The former was a group of chaplains, clerks and choristers who travelled with him from one royal residence to another, maintaining daily divine worship, and the latter was a large body mainly of instrumentalists who provided secular entertainment in the household and played for masques.

Cardinal Wolsey was likewise a patron of the arts. His chapel was equipped on no less lavish a scale than that of the Monarch himself, and the quality of the music matched the elaborate ritual and surroundings, a foretaste of the splendour that was later to characterize his new foundation at Oxford.

Musicians employed in Court circles or in the service of the Papal Legate enjoyed comfort and security, and had every opportunity for developing and practising their art. Those who did not manage to secure these coveted positions would find ready employment in one of the hundred or more churches and religious foundations within the bounds of the City. Here chaplains, clerks and choristers would find permanent appointments, and conducts and laymen would be in constant demand to assist on feast days and other special occasions.

It is therefore obvious, from this brief survey alone, that London would be a strong temptation to a young composer of provincial and rural origin. If in fact Taverner did spend some time in the metropolis during the early sixteenth century, he would certainly have had every opportunity of hearing a wide variety of musical styles, and of meeting the leading composers of the day. There is no record of his having held a post at Court or in Wolsey's Chapel, and unfortunately only a small proportion of the London church accounts of the day have been preserved, none of which gives any hint of a Taverner appointment. It has been suggested that he might have worked as a conduct — that is, hiring himself out on daily or short term contracts, augmenting the permanent staff of a church for special services and celebrations. In this freelance capacity he would have been able to follow a wider range of pursuits than if he had been tied to one particular establishment.

All this is admittedly conjecture, but a more convincing argument in favour of Taverner's supposed London sojourn stems from the discovery of some of his music in four early sixteenth-century manuscripts. The first one comes from Henry VIII's extensive collection and appears to have been originally prepared for the Chapel Royal. It takes the form of five large, elaborately presented part-books of which only the contratenor and bassus have survived.[9] They contain masses and other sacred works by Hugh Aston, Richard Davy, and Robert Fayrfax together with two large-scale Votive Antiphons, *Ave Dei patris filia* and *Gaude plurimum* by John Taverner. These same two works appear unattributed in another manuscript of the time that originally belonged to the Chapel Royal, and comprised a set of small, less elaborately presented part-books, of which only the meane has survived.[10] Again the Taverner works are in company with motets by Davy, Fayrfax, Ludford, Pygot and other contemporary writers. From the composers represented and the predominance of Marian settings, — *Salve Regina, Virgo templum*, etc. — there is good reason to believe that both these manuscripts date from sometime between 1515 and 1525.

A third Taverner work, the *Western Wind* Mass, is represented by an extract from the opening of the *Agnus Dei* which appears in one of two small complementary manuscripts[11] together containing a miscellaneous collection of secular songs, antiphons, motets and instrumental pieces. These manuscripts are thought to be the work of a musician who was associated with the English Court shortly before 1520. Although this is not the place for a detailed examination of the Mass,[12] there are melodic and stylistic reasons for placing it early in the composer's career, and the estimated dating and provenance of the manuscript in which the extract appears point to it having been written in London.

Finally a group of secular songs commands our attention. Taverner is generally regarded exclusively as a church composer, and certainly forty or more of his extant works fall into this sacred category, but his settings of four love lyrics appear in a book of *XX Songes* printed in London in October, 1530. Unfortunately only the bass part[13] along with fragments of the treble

9 Cambridge University Library, MS. Dd. 13. 27, and St John's College, Cambridge MS. K. 31.
10 British Museum, Harleian MS. 1709.
11 British Museum, MS. Royal App. 56.
12 See pp. 55ff.
13 British Museum, K. 1. e. 1.

and meane[14] have survived from the original four books. Nevertheless, the one complete song, *In Women Is Rest Peas And Pacience*, together with a substantial part of each of the other three settings, is sufficient to indicate that they were probably written in London in the early sixteenth century. Even though the dating of the manuscript does not help us greatly, the style of the songs clearly bears the stamp of Tudor Court circles, reminding us of similar works contained in such collections as the Fayrfax Book (c.1500) and Henry VIII's Book (c.1515).

Already there is mounting evidence to support the theory that Taverner did spend part of his early life in London, but these pointers also raise the question as to why his potential should not have been recognised sufficiently to secure for him a post at Henry's Court. It is possible that he chose to remain a freelance musician, or even held a congenial church appointment of which we have no record. In a dissertation by Hugh Benham,[15] the author is unable to accept the theory of a London sojourn, and feels more inclined to believe that Taverner was educated at Tattershall College, and then stayed on after his days as a chorister were over. Why, Benham asks, should a young composer after savouring the musical opportunities of the metropolis 'return to a place as comparatively remote as Tattershall', turning his back upon the City and all that it could offer?

There is admittedly some validity in this argument, but we must not underestimate the importance of Lord Cromwell's foundation in South Lincolnshire. The history of the place which has already been traced should be sufficient to indicate that Tattershall was far from being a provincial backwater, even if in later years it fell into obscurity. It lay on a direct route between Boston and the City of Lincoln, namely the River Witham. In Tudor times, Boston was the third port in the kingdom outside London, and its river link with the hinterland was a busy thoroughfare for merchandise. With this also came an interchange of ideas and every kind of Continental influence. We have already discovered the opportunities, musical and otherwise, offered by the College itself, so that Taverner's return from London to his possible place of birth would not be the retrograde step that has been suggested.

It is difficult to determine the precise date of his return, for the annual calendar of the St Nicholas Gild listed only new and deceased members, and no record is made of resignations, promotions or transfers from one appointment to another. There is

14 Westminster Abbey Library.
15 Southampton University, 1969.

no mention of either John Taverner or his wife Annes between their election to membership in 1514 and the year 1521 when the Bede Roll suddenly comes to an end. All we can deduce from this document, therefore, is that both were alive in 1520, the last year of recorded deaths, though it does not follow that Taverner was still in employment in London or that either of them was still resident in the City. It has been suggested by some scholars that Taverner returned to his native Lincolnshire in the early 1520s, following the death of his wife. Whilst there is at present no evidence to support this theory, it could prove to be a perfectly feasible explanation, for we do know that the clerk-fellow at Tattershall was contemplating marriage in 1526. Assuming for the moment that he and the London Taverner were one and the same person, he must have left the capital sometime between 1521 and 1525. However, it is certain that John Taverner, the composer, was in residence at Tattershall College in the Spring of 1525, after which we are back on *terra firma*, secure in the knowledge that reliable documentation exists for at least the next five years of his life.

The year in which we find the name of John Taverner recorded as a clerk-fellow at Tattershall was the same one in which Cardinal Wolsey issued a charter for the building of a new college at Oxford. Following the ambitious scheme that characterized the staffing and equipping of his personal chapel and the ordering of his palace at Hampton Court, Cardinal College (as it became known) was conceived on a scale that spared neither effort nor expense. The new College was built on the site of a former Augustinian Priory, St Frideswide's, which had been suppressed by the Papal Legate to make way for his dream project. Revenues from the Priory, together with monies that accumulated as a result of the dissolution of several small monastic houses in different parts of the land, helped to finance Wolsey's scheme, which was launched in the early part of 1525. The Dean, John Higden, had already been appointed, and in July of that year the foundation stone was laid by Bishop Longland.

The College complex was to comprise a large quadrangle, a fine library, an imposing great hall, and a chapel to rival King's College, Cambridge. The building programme under Dean Higden and Nicholas Townley, Master of the Works, proceeded with such rapidity and purpose that by the end of 1526 lodgings on two sides of the quadrangle had been completed, together with the kitchen and servants' quarters. More than that, the hall was in an advanced stage of building, and the foundations of the chapel and cloisters had been laid.

The statutes of the College, which was dedicated to the Holy Trinity, St Frideswide and All Saints, were drawn up early in 1525 by Wolsey, assisted by Thomas Cromwell, Earl of Essex, and Stephen Gardiner, Bishop of Winchester. These made provision for the appointment of a dean (already chosen), sixty fellows or senior canons, forty junior scholars, and professors in humanity, law, medicine, philosophy and theology. No time was lost in staffing Cardinal College, and by the end of July 1526 the first eighteen canons had been named.[16] Furthermore, the statutes went on to provide a body of men and boys to assist mainly in chapel so that divine worship could be maintained with dignity and regularity. The chapel staff consisted of thirteen chaplains, twelve clerks skilled in polyphony, one of whom would act as organist, and sixteen choristers presided over by an *informator* or choirmaster.

In the Autumn of 1525, Dr Robert Shorton of Cambridge University was appointed Wolsey's Dean of Chapel, and with him came a group of brilliant young scholars, many of whom achieved distinction in later life. They brought with them the seeds of progressive and liberal thought based upon the beliefs of the prophet Erasmus of Rotterdam. It was he who had earlier prepared an edition of the New Testament which differed from the teaching of the Vulgate, and questioned certain aspects of Papal rule and authority. At the time, Cambridge was known as the centre of the so-called 'new learning', a movement that was gaining support, and on the transference to Oxford of Robert Shorton and his young scholars a new centre was thereby established. In little more than two years this movement was to erupt, spreading its heretical ideas amongst a college community that was already building for itself an otherwise healthy reputation. Before investigating this episode in the history of Cardinal College, however, another appointment to the chapel there must first be described: the post of Master of the Choristers.

This task fell to the lot of John Longland, Bishop of Lincoln. He first invited a musician from Newark College, Leicester[17] who, we are informed,[18] declined the offer on the grounds of already having 'in perpetuity' a secure and well-paid post. The Bishop then

16 Oxford Historical Society, Vol. VIII, pp. 58-9.
17 Identified as Hugh Aston (Harrison, *Music in Medieval Britain*).
18 In a letter from Wolsey to Bishop Longland dated 4 September 1526, and preserved in the Public Record Office, London, MS. S. P. 1/39, f. 118.

approached John Taverner, who was of course at this time a clerk-fellow at Tattershall. Initially he met with no success, and in a letter to Wolsey[19] explained that his invitation had not been accepted since Taverner 'allegeth the assurance and profit of his living at Tattershall and that he is in way of a good marriage which he should lose if he did remove from thence'. Frustrated in his efforts to fill the post at Oxford, Longland went on in his letter to suggest that a temporary appointment be made from amongst the resident staff of the chapel so that Wolsey's plans to celebrate the Feast of St Frideswide (19 October) should go ahead with due pomp and ceremony.

It is difficult to understand Taverner's apparent lack of ambition in refusing so prestigious and so lucrative a post as that at the Cardinal's chapel, though one can appreciate the concern about his proposed marriage, his second if we accept the London episode. Without indulging in conjecture, one might be tempted to regard his decision as some kind of excuse. Perhaps he felt inadequate to the task, or unsuited to life in such exalted academic circles. On the other hand, he might well have been happy in his work at Tattershall, enjoying relative security and reluctant to pull up roots and face the unknown. Whatever his reasons, he must nevertheless have had a speedy change of heart, for within the space of a month he had accepted the invitation, and by November 1526 had been appointed *Informator Choristorum* at Cardinal College.

Wolsey obviously attached considerable importance to the post of choirmaster, for it was the highest salaried position in the College after the Dean, the Sub-dean and the professors. In all it carried an annual sum of ten pounds plus a further five pounds for general expenses, described in the College account book[20] as 'livery and commons'. In return, the list of qualifications required of an *informator* was a formidable one. According to Bishop Longland's letter already quoted,[21] it included ability in singing and organ-playing, a wide knowledge of music suitable for all occasions in the church year, competence in training choristers, and a certain flair for the general administration of the choir.

When Taverner took up his appointment, the College was already functioning in the midst of an ambitious building pro-

19 Dated 17 October 1526, and preserved in the Public Record Office, London, MS. S. P. 1/39, f. 139.
20 Public Record Office, London: Treasury of Receipt of the Exchequer, Misc. books, E/36/102. f. 4.
21 Footnote 19 above.

gramme, and new staff were continually arriving to join the community. He was installed in a chapel that had previously been equipped with a splendid array of vestments brought from Hampton Court, and a collection of service books that Wolsey had acquired as a result of the suppression of various religious houses in different parts of the country. Taverner therefore had every opportunity of building a musical tradition to match the standards elsewhere in the College, and in this he was backed by a patron who spared no expense in the fulfilment of these aims. Days at Tattershall might at times have made heavy demands upon him, but now in sole charge, and carrying the musical responsibility for a thriving chapel community, life must indeed have been full.

In accordance with the Statutes of the College, the day's devotions began at 5 am with the choristers chanting Marian Matins. This was immediately followed by First Matins and Prime sung to plainsong by the chaplains and clerks. Then came the Mass of the Blessed Virgin Mary, and after it a Requiem Mass, both in polyphonic settings. To complete the morning's devotions, the Mass for the Day was sung by the full choir.

Chapel duties were resumed in the afternoon at three o'clock with Marian Vespers said by the choristers, followed by Office Vespers and Compline sung to plainchant by the men of the choir. Then three antiphons were sung in polyphonic settings, the first to the Trinity, the second to the Blessed Virgin, and the third to St William, a twelfth-century Archbishop of York who was canonised in 1226. Finally at seven o'clock the full choir sang *Salve Regina*, *Ave Maria* and the antiphon *Sancte Deus*, again each in polyphony. Certain days also saw the commemoration in song of the Trinity, St Frideswide and All Saints. In addition to this regular pattern of worship, the entire College community met weekly to observe funeral rites for Wolsey's parents and to pray for the future salvation of the souls of Wolsey himself and the Monarchy.

We have no record of any specific music used during these early days at Cardinal College, but it is inevitable that a wide variety of masses, motets and antiphons would be performed during the course of so ambitious a chapel programme, and we may be certain that some of the works would be written by the *Informator* for his own use. There is no evidence to support the statement made by E. H. Fellowes that Taverner 'wrote all his fine church music' during the short time he was at Oxford.[22] On the contrary,

22 *Grove's Dictionary of Music and Musicians*, Vol. VIII, p. 323.

the very varied nature of his output would indicate that it was composed over a very much longer period. Certain works, however, do clearly belong to his Oxford years, especially the three six-part Festal Masses that were copied at Cardinal College during his lifetime. Similarly the Votive Antiphon, *Jesu Christe pastor bone* and the Mass *Sancti Wilhelmi* or *Small Devotion*, which was probably written in commemoration of the Feast of St William of York, also bear the Oxford stamp. Finally, the settings of *Ave Maria* and *Sancte Deus* no doubt date from the same period since these texts were used regularly, according to the College Statutes, towards the end of each day's devotions.

It was early in his second year at Oxford that Taverner became marginally involved in the activities of a dissident underground movement sparked off by John Clark, one of the ex-Cambridge scholars and an exponent of the 'new learning'. His daily lectures in Lutheran theology attracted a group of followers from amongst the liberal-minded members of the academic staff, and he also found a sympathetic audience in some of the chapel community. One such person was unfortunately the choirmaster himself — unfortunate because of the effect it had upon his future reputation. It was this involvement which, in the hands of John Foxe, assumed such exaggerated proportions that a chronicle of events grew from it which came to be looked upon as fact. Taverner's interest in Lutheran teaching was interpreted as his conversion to Protestantism, and his subsequent departure from Oxford was assumed to be occasioned by this change of heart. Next, his supposed abandonment of composition was regarded as proof of his renunciation of the Roman faith, and all this was then linked with his later life in Boston when he acted as an agent for Thomas Cromwell in the suppression of religious houses in South Lincolnshire, thereby earning the title of a 'fierce fanatic'.[23] This image has become widely believed and accepted, even to the extent of providing in recent years a plot for an opera on the composer's life by Peter Maxwell Davies; but, as will be seen, it is far from reality.

To return to the roots of this narrative, Clark's lectures on the 'new learning' soon spread beyond the bounds of Cardinal College, and found adherents in other Oxford houses. They included a young scholar named Anthony Dalaber, of St Alban's Hall and later of Gloucester College. It was he who, towards the end of his life, recounted the heresy affair to John Foxe, and Foxe in

23 According to E. H. Fellowes.

turn recorded the events in his *Acts and Monuments*, adding his own deductions and comments.

It appears that, at the same time as John Clark was expounding his progressive thought in Oxford, two London book agents, John Gough and Robert Farman, were importing copies of Tyndale's translation of the New Testament together with anti-papal literature and Lutheran tracts, and distributing them in various parts of the country, principally the strongholds of the 'new learning' in Cambridge, the South-West and the metropolis. Some of these books found their way to Oxford through the agency of a dissident cleric named Thomas Garret. Towards the end of 1527 he was suspected of assisting John Clark in the dissemination of Protestant ideologies, and a close watch was kept on his movements, culminating in his arrest and interrogation. In his ultimate confession of guilt he named a long list of accomplices, including Anthony Dalaber, who had attempted to engineer Garret's escape from justice and who had earlier bought heretical literature from him. When in turn Dalaber was questioned about *his* part in the conspiracy, we are told that 'he betrayed twenty-two of his associates'.[24] During the course of the ensuing investigation, several of the scholars at Cardinal College were found to be in possession of Protestant literature, and a search revealed a number of Garret's books concealed in the rooms of both Radley, a clerk of chapel, and Taverner.

The offenders were then brought before Dean Higden for questioning, and, according to John Foxe, 'were therefore accused of heresy unto the cardinal, and cast into prison' — actually into the foul confines of the College salt-fish cellar. Foxe then goes on to say that 'Taverner, although he was accused and suspected for hiding of Clark's books under the boards in his school; yet the cardinal for his music excused him, saying that he was but a musician: and so he escaped'. Then comes the famous marginal note saying how Taverner regretted having 'made songs to popish ditties in the time of his blindness'.[25]

This account is both inaccurate and misleading, for it gives the impression that Taverner was first thrown into prison together with the other dissenters, and later released by the Cardinal. Furthermore, the final marginal comment has for long come to be regarded as evidence that he abandoned composition altogether after his involvement in the heresy case. The situation is partly

24 Maxwell Lyte: *History of the University of Oxford* (1886), p. 465.
25 *Acts and Monuments*, p. 251.

clarified, however, in a letter[26] written by John Higden to Wolsey's chaplain, Thomas Byrton, in which he lists the names of the scholars whom, 'according to His Grace's command' he had 'kept in ward'. He then goes on to say: 'As for Master Taverner I have not commit him to prison, neither Radley' because 'they be unlearned, and not to be regarded'. This last phrase should not be taken too literally, for it must surely mean that these two members of the chapel were less knowledgeable in Lutheran doctrine than the accused scholars, and therefore, in their duties, less dangerously placed to be a risk in the community. In summary the Dean then adds: 'As for Master Taverner, the hiding of Master Clark's books and being privy to the letter sent to Master Clark from Master Garret after he was fled be the greatest things after my mind that can be laid to his charge'. Regarding Foxe's marginal comment, Taverner's continued activities at Cardinal College are alone sufficient to refute any suggestion that he abandoned composition after this incident.

It is obvious that Wolsey did not regard Taverner's part in the heresy affair as a heinous crime. Had he done so, he would most certainly have dismissed him from the high position that he held, for he had even excommunicated some of the prime dissidents in the College. Instead we find the *Informator* immediately resuming his duties, and the chapel quickly returning to normal. It is interesting to note that at this time Taverner's abilities were recognised beyond the bounds of Oxford, for, in a letter to Wolsey,[27] Thomas Cromwell declared that he had found the chapel 'most devoutly and virtuously ordered' and 'the service daily done within the same so devout, solemn, and full of harmony, that it hath few peers'.

During the remaining two years that Taverner was at Oxford, he continued to enjoy the approval and support of his patron, and even assisted him in the staffing of the chapel choir at his new foundation at Ipswich. This was a college of secular canons that Wolsey had established in his birthplace as a nursery where scholars were trained for places at Cardinal College. Begun in spring 1528 on the grandiose scale that we have come to associate with its founder, it was almost fully staffed by late summer that year, and the chapel was ceremoniously opened in September. In

26 Letter dated 15 March 1528, Public Record Office, London, MS. S. P. 1/47, f. 111.
27 H. Ellis (Ed.), *Original Papers Illustrative of English History*, 3rd Series (1846), Vol. II, p. 139.

a letter[28] written by Nicholas Townley, Master of Works at Cardinal College, to Thomas Alvard, a gentleman in Wolsey's service, we read of Taverner accompanying the Cardinal to Hampton Court for the purpose of auditioning choristers, two of whom were required for transfer to the new college. It is significant that the staffing of the lesser foundation at Ipswich was carried out with the same care as had been exercised previously at Oxford, even though at the time Wolsey must have been preoccupied with the political problems that were shortly to lead to his fall from grace. Had not these problems precipitated themselves with such speed and severity, it is likely that Taverner would have enjoyed a prolonged period of service at Cardinal College.

His stay, however, proved to be shorter than he probably anticipated, for Wolsey's failure to secure an annulment of Henry's marriage to Catherine of Aragon led to a rapid decline in his popularity at Court, and to his final downfall in October 1529. This was the end. He resigned his Chancellorship and was relieved of his various titles, and his foundations at Hampton Court, Oxford, Ipswich and York Place, London became Crown property. Of the two collegiate establishments, Ipswich held little interest for the King, probably because of its very personal associations with the deposed Cardinal, and less than eighteen months after the foundation stone had been laid the machinery was already in motion for its suppression.

Meanwhile, morale was at a low level at Oxford, for rumours had reached the community that it was to suffer a similar fate to that of its younger relation at Ipswich. In the end, however, Henry decided to re-found the College in accordance with his own wishes, though this did not come about until July 1532, and the intervening period of uncertainty contributed to a marked fall in its membership, both academic and chapel. It was at this point that Taverner, witnessing the decline of an establishment which only months earlier had been the symbol of scholarship and religious ceremonial, decided that the time had come to leave. With a depleted choir, reduced resources, and perhaps a threat of redundancy, there was every reason for seeking fresh opportunities, and in April 1530 at the end of Hilary Term, he resigned his position at the College. Records tell us that he was paid five pounds for two terms' service,[29] and, after a three-month interregnum during which the choir was administered by two chaplains, he was succeeded by a certain John Benbow from Manchester.

28 Public Record Office, London, MS. S.P. Henry VIII, 235, f. 290.
29 *Letters & Papers of the Reign of Henry VIII*, H.M.S.O.

His departure from Oxford was therefore due to purely practical considerations, and, contrary to what has been recorded by
some music historians, was not connected with any change in his
own religious convictions. There is also every reason to believe
that Taverner continued to compose both immediately after the
heresy episode and during his post-Oxford years. Whilst April
1530 then marks the end of a chapter in his working life, there is
no evidence to suggest that it marked the end of his creative
career.

For the six years following his departure from Oxford,
Taverner's whereabouts have been, and still are, a complete
mystery. His decision to leave Cardinal College appears to have
been a fairly hasty one, and we can only assume that some new
opportunity had presented itself that might have been missed
had he stayed to complete the academic year. The situation has
obviously led to speculation, and the two most popular theories
are that he moved either to a musical appointment in London or
back to his native Lincolnshire. There is no evidence in support of
the former suggestion, but if we accept that he did spend some
time in his early life as a freelance musician in the capital, it is
possible that he could have returned there in a similar capacity.
It is doubtful if he accepted a post at Court, and equally unlikely
that he took up any church position remotely like the one he had
held at Cardinal College, for there would surely have been some
record of such an appointment or some evidence of his subsequent
activities therein.

The other suggestion, that he might have immediately returned
to South Lincolnshire, is partly based upon the next known
reference to him when his name appears in the 1537 list of new
members of the Gild of Corpus Christi in Boston.[30] Doubt has
been cast upon this argument, however, because it is hardly
possible that a person of Taverner's reputation should have been
allowed to reside in the area for more than six years before being
elected to Gild membership. We must therefore assume that his
move to Boston did not occur before the middle of the decade,
and, until more positive evidence comes to light, this period must
remain an enigma.

The last eight years of his life (1537-45) are relatively well
documented, though a certain misinterpretation of records has
resulted in a picture that is far from accurate, and even detri-
mental to Taverner's image. The main sources of information for

30   The Register is in the British Museum, London, Harleian MS. 4795.

these years are the gild register already mentioned, the *Inquisition post mortem* of 1546, and his widow's will (1553). To these can be added letters from Taverner to Thomas Cromwell, which give some insight into the composer's character, and an incomplete document which contains some details of his widow's descendants.

The register of the Gild of Corpus Christi provides a starting point from which we learn that Taverner was a married man when admitted to membership in 1537, his wife being Rose Parrowe, a Boston widow and daughter of a man of local repute, himself a member of the Gild. She had two daughters, Emma and Isabel, by her previous marriage. It is most unlikely that she was the same person as the one Taverner was contemplating marrying when, as a clerk at Tattershall in 1526, he first declined the invitation to Cardinal College. There is no record of the date of their marriage, but as Rose Parrowe had only recently been widowed at the time of the entry in the Gild Register, circumstances would suggest somewhere around 1536. This placing is further supported by the fact that, in the following year, Taverner transferred the titles of lands that he had acquired in Boston from his own name to joint ownership with his wife.

The Lincolnshire town to which Taverner came sometime in the early or middle 1530s was a thriving community, having grown up as a focal point for trade between Central England and the Continent. Geographically placed as it was, with a direct inland waterway link, it became one of the wealthiest ports in the country. The town itself developed on both sides of the River Witham, with warehouses lining its banks. Around its huge market place and beyond, there sprang up imposing dwellings built by prosperous merchants for their families, and financed by a highly profitable trade in wool, corn, timber, farming products and miscellaneous goods of every kind. In due course, the town centre became dominated by an enormous Parish Church, the famous Boston Stump, which was completed towards the end of the fifteenth century. According to contemporary sources, its musical services were of a high order. Wealthy families of repute encouraged the influx of preaching friars, who began to arrive as early as the mid-thirteenth century, and established four communities in the town.

Gilds were founded, starting life as fraternities, each bound together by a common occupation. As time went on, their interests widened beyond their original functions as friendly societies, and they became increasingly responsible for the welfare of the townspeople at large. They ceased to be associated with particular

29

occupations, and some of them drew their membership from a variety of trades and professions. It was these groups who ultimately governed the town and from whose ranks its aldermen and leading officials were elected. Their guildhalls became places in which policies affecting the community were debated and decided, and those who held office were men of influence in the town. They assumed responsibility for law and order, for the maintenance of public buildings and amenities, and for the smooth running of the port facilities themselves. In addition to all these materialistic features, they were diligent in their religious observances, maintaining chapels in their guildhalls, and, in some cases, altars in the Parish Church of St Botolph. They also attended to the needs of the families of deceased members, hiring chaplains to conduct funeral services and to pray for the repose of departed souls.

The two largest and most important gilds were the Marian and Corpus Christi, and every Boston citizen of any standing was a member of one or both of them. The former, founded in 1260, was the older, and its membership in Tudor times included Thomas Garret who had earlier been involved in the Oxford heresy affair, and who was now a master in the grammar school maintained by the Gild. Also connected with the fraternity was John Wendon, clerk and organist at the Gild Chapel, and Richard Gillmyn, a chaplain, who were both close friends and associates of Taverner. We have no record of Taverner's own membership as the complete register has been lost, and the surviving pages list only some of those who held office.

The Boston Gild of Corpus Christi, however, is more fully documented. It was founded in 1335 by a group of thirty men (including by coincidence a certain Taverner) and its early constitution made provision for six chaplains whose duties were to pray for the King, his Court and the members of the Gild. Its membership drew from a wide variety of occupations, though the relatively high entry fee of £2-4s-4d quoted in the records of 1426 led to a large proportion of merchants and tradesmen within its ranks. By Taverner's time, most Boston people of note were listed in its register, and some were admitted as honorary members. The Gild grew in size and prosperity, and with resources accruing from its ownership of lands and properties in the area it was able to provide financially for the daily needs of twelve poor men in the town. It maintained a chapel in the Parish Church and a group of clergymen to fulfil its religious obligations, which included the appropriate recognition of the Feast of Corpus Christi.

There is no indication that Taverner made any contribution to the activities of the Gild, or, for that matter, to any other organisation in Boston. As will be seen later, his duties as a Crown agent during the years 1538 to 1540 would prevent his accepting any simultaneous musical appointment, and the positions to which he later rose in the civic life of the community would not allow him to take part in services either as a hired clerk or a conduct. Nevertheless, one would imagine that he might have used his creative talents in some direction, perhaps even providing new music for special services and commemorations.

After the initial entry in the Gild Register, Taverner's name next appears in 1541 when he became treasurer, an office that he held until records ceased three years later. In February 1545, Boston was incorporated as a Borough, and on 1 June the Mayor, Nyclas Robartson, was publicly sworn in. After him 'the xij alderman of the said Borough, that is . . . John Taverner, . . . did take their corporate oaths'.[31] If we examine the Council Minutes of the next few years, we find that most of these first twelve aldermen in turn became Mayor of Boston, and there is every possibility that Taverner would in due course have been elected to that office had he not died in October 1545 after only five months' service to the new Borough.

To return to the previous decade, however, we find Taverner employed in a capacity that earned for him the reputation of being a cruel persecutor of the pre-Reformation Church which he had earlier served so diligently. In this respect he is once again the victim of a myth that has been handed down from one writer to another, and which immediately explodes when we examine the situation in its context, together with some of his surviving correspondence.

The sequence of events begins in the early 1530s, possibly before Taverner moved to Boston, and partly stems from King Henry's attempts to replenish his financial resources which had fallen to an alarmingly low level. In hasty consultations, it was decided that the Church might be an easy source of revenue, and the quickest way of increasing Crown reserves. Thomas Cromwell was therefore ordered to make an exhaustive survey of every church, monastery, friary and other religious establishment in the land. The result was a comprehensive account produced in 1534 under the title of *Valor Ecclesiasticus*[32] which showed the

31 The complete list of aldermen is recorded in the *Council Minutes*, Vol. I f. 55, in Boston Town Hall.
32 Caley & Hunter (Ed.) in six volumes, London Record Commission.

income for each of these foundations. This document revealed an immediate potential source of revenue, but it also drew attention to a large number of religious houses that were understaffed and whose income was inadequate for their day-to-day requirements. Despite their poverty, however, some of these establishments had considerable wealth in the form of chapel property, including vestments, plate, papal symbols and relics. An Act of Parliament passed early in 1536 made possible the suppression of the smaller monastic foundations, and the following year some of the larger houses were forced to forfeit their valuables in the interests of the Crown treasury. Henry's excuse for this course of action was that religious establishments were still maintaining allegiance to the Pope instead of to him. 1537 also saw the initial measures taken in the dissolution of the friaries, which, like many of the smaller monastic houses, had fallen into decline through a lack of income and the loss of some of the patronage that they had previously enjoyed. It is in this connection that we find Taverner working as an agent for Thomas Cromwell, the man who had earlier recognised the composer's abilities when he visited Cardinal College in 1528.

The friars who had begun to arrive in this country during the thirteenth century belonged to four Orders — the Augustinians, the Carmelites, the Dominicans and the Franciscans — and each established a community in Boston, three on the east side of the river and one on the west. Even though they never possessed the wealth associated with some of the monasteries, they all enjoyed the support of the more prosperous families of the area who had originally encouraged them to come to this country. As time went on, however, the initial enthusiasm of their patrons began to wane, and by the early sixteenth century their life had become a mere existence and their lot pitiable. Furthermore their beliefs and practices were deeply rooted in papal doctrine and superstition which did not find sympathy with the King. It was therefore decided to suppress them, not simply for financial gain, but because such a move would at least contribute towards tidying up the Church and ridding it of an unwelcome element.

In the Autumn of 1538, Taverner started work on the Boston friaries which, when he visited them, he found to be in a sorrowful state. The four communities had each been compelled to sell most of its relatively few chapel possessions — plate and the like — in order to survive, and, with very few saleable commodities left, the future for them looked bleak. It is in this situation that we discover Taverner, not as a cruel persecutor, but as a compassionate individual, sufficiently concerned about the welfare of the friars to write to Cromwell on their behalf. In a letter dated 20 January 1539,[33] he reports to his employer on the conditions under which they had been living, and how they had approached him 'lamenting their great poverty knowing no manner of ways how to provide livings for them and their poor brethren till such time as their houses be surrendered'. He goes on: 'the devotion of the people is clean gone, their plate and other implements be sold and the money spent so that in manner there is nothing left to make sale of now but only lead[34] which if I had not given them contrary commandment they would likewise have plucked down and sold to have relieved therewith them and their poor brethren. But in avoiding such spoil I bade them come to me in meanwhile at all times when they lacked anything and they should have it of me.' He then appeals to Cromwell: '. . . I humbly beseech Your good Lordship that they may know your pleasure and commandment by my servant [the bearer of the letter] what they shall do.'

This letter presents a totally different picture of Taverner from the one painted by most writers, for it shows him exercising his duties with a degree of human concern that was noticeably absent in the attitude of Crown agents in other parts of the country. In this respect alone it is a valuable document, but it also links up with another letter dated 11 September 1538, again to Cromwell, which throws a little light upon Taverner's religious views at the time. In this letter the writer reports that 'According to Your Lordship's command the rood was burned the 7th day of this month being also the market day, and a sermon of the Black Friar at the burning of him, who did express the cause of his burning and the idolatry committed by him, which sermon hath done much good and hath turned many men's hearts from it'.[35]

For a long time this passage has been misinterpreted, and the author's actions attributed to a 'fanatic', driven to these ends 'under pressure of religious conviction'.[36] Taken in its context, however, this is far from the truth. Although Taverner was simply carrying out his employer's instructions, he was not simultaneously indulging in open rebellion against the church. Rather, his disagreement was with the superstitions and trappings that had for so long surrounded Roman belief and doctrine. His organising

33 *Letters & Papers of Henry VIII*, Vol. CXLII, ff. 101-2, London Public Record Office.
34 That is, roofing lead.
35 *Letters & Papers of Henry VIII*, Vol. CXXXVI, ff. 133-4, London Public Record Office.
36 E. H. Fellowes.

of the public burning of the Rood — the huge cross that had hung beneath the chancel arch in the Parish Church — was clearly a symbolic act against papal idolatry and superfluous practices connected with the church. Equally his part in the suppression of the friaries was conducted, not in a spirit of religious persecution, but as a practical step towards releasing poverty-stricken communities from the papal bonds in which they were held. What therefore appears on the surface to be a flowering of the seeds planted during the heresy incident at Oxford some ten years earlier gives way to a much simpler and more realistic explanation. It also helps to account for the respect that Taverner must have enjoyed in his last years, both in the office of treasurer of the Gild of Corpus Christi and in the civic life of Boston as an elected member of the aldermanic bench.

So far his will has not been traced, but two documents, the composer's *Inquisition post mortem*[37] and his widow's will[38] throw some light on these final years. Taverner appears to have relinquished his duties as a Crown agent in 1540, and spent the remainder of his life serving the town and community in which he lived. He was by this time a man of moderate means, not wealthy, but capable of maintaining a comfortable home for himself and his wife. Prior to his marriage to Rose Parrowe, he had bought farming land to the value of about ninety pounds, and at his death, he left three and a half acres in Boston itself, together with twenty-eight acres of arable land and pasture in Skirbeck, an area near the town.

According to the above-mentioned documents, Taverner died in Boston on 18 October 1545, and was buried under the bell-tower of the Parish Church. Eight years later, in May 1553, Rose Taverner died, willing that she too 'be buried in the Parish Church of St Botolph in the said Boston in the bell house next my husband'.[39] Apart from a few miscellaneous household goods and clothing which she left to her brother, John Parrowe, and to her two sisters, Agnes and Alice, most of her possessions together with the property of her late husband were bequeathed to her two daughters, 'that is to say, Isabel Hodge wife of Richard Hodge and the heirs of her body lawfully begotten and to Emma Salmon the

37 Taken at Donington, a small town ten miles from Boston, on 5 October 1546.
38 Dated 1 May 1553.
39 Lincoln Archive Office, *Consistory Court Wills*, 1551-53, f. 271, and 1552-56, f. 177.

wife of Steven Salmon and the heirs of her body lawfully begotten forever, and for lack of such issue it to be sold and disposed in deeds of charity at the discretion of mine executors'.[40]

Taverner's resting place remains unmarked, and the visitor to the Parish Church of St Botolph will search in vain for any commemorative tablet or plaque. We are fortunate, however, in that a substantial number of his works have survived intact, and these in themselves are sufficient memorial.

What kind of a person then was John Taverner?

As to his appearance, there is little to help us beyond a number of facial drawings that are incorporated into the initial letters of the text in the manuscript of the Mass, *Gloria tibi Trinitas*.[41] These outlines, depicting a man with a protruding forehead, a mis-shapen nose, and a slightly pugilistic expression, are almost certainly those of the composer. On the other hand we have sufficient biographical information to build up a fairly clear picture of his character, and from the foregoing survey two salient features emerge. First, one must completely reject the traditional image of Taverner as a man who, under the influence of Protestantism, turned to a career of religious persecution. This is totally unacceptable. It does not take into account the period of continued service at Cardinal College following the heresy involvement, nor the assistance given to Wolsey in finding suitable choristers for the new foundation at Ipswich; it is not consistent with membership of the Gild of Corpus Christi which was, after all, a Catholic-based organisation, maintaining chapels in its guildhall and in the Parish Church; it does not correspond with the generosity extended towards the friars of Boston at the time of their suppression, and it makes nonsense of his burial in the very church that was the object of his supposed harassment.

Evidence not only fails to support this image but points in an entirely different direction, and it is only when we examine all available information to date that we discover a man rebelling, not against the church itself, but against malpractices associated with it. In short, Taverner saw the symbols and superstitions — the rood, the figures and the relics — all standing in the way of its real purpose. There was no question of his rejecting the faith in which he had grown up and worked, or of casting overboard his former religious beliefs in favour of newly-acquired ideas. He was

40 *Ibid.*
41 In the Forrest-Heyther part-books, q.v.

simply reacting against the idolatry that had become so closely connected with Roman ritual. He fully recognised the need for reform, and in this respect alone he shared common ground with Luther himself, but reform within the bounds of his own church, and not along the lines of the 'new learning' he had experienced at Oxford. It is unfortunate that Taverner's efforts to eradicate what he saw to be obstacles to worship should have coincided with his activities as a Crown agent, and it is equally regrettable that the burning of the Rood in Boston Market Place should have been regarded in isolation by some historians as an act of religious persecution. The result has been a long-accepted and totally inaccurate picture of the man, but when the subject is examined in full context and with all documentary evidence to hand we discover Taverner still embracing his original faith, and a figure of the 'Establishment' to the end of his days.

The second point concerns his supposed abandonment of composition in the wake of newly-acquired religious beliefs which were the result of involvement in the Oxford heresy. Once again, we have a theory based upon inadequate and possibly unreliable information. In this case it is the already-quoted marginal statement by John Foxe which says that Taverner 'repented him very much that he had made songs to popish ditties in the time of his blindness'.[42] It should be recalled that Foxe's narrative was based upon an account of the Oxford affair given to him by a participant, Anthony Dalaber, some thirty years after the event, by which time details could have been forgotten, and facts exaggerated and distorted. Nevertheless, this statement was immediately seized upon by music historians as evidence of a change of heart on the part of the composer, a rejection of his former beliefs, and a conversion to Protestantism. This image has already been refuted, but the phrase 'popish ditties' is still of sufficient interest to command attention.

The most convincing explanation is the one advanced by Denis Stevens who suggests[43] that it might refer specifically to settings of Marian texts. This is all the more acceptable when we consider it in relation to Taverner's later efforts to purge the church of its superfluities. Did he at this stage regard the traditional antiphons to the Blessed Virgin Mary as unnecessary trappings, standing in the way of direct worship expressed through the Mass? Was this the point in his life when he first became aware of the changes

42 Foxe, *Acts and Monuments*, (1583), p. 1032.
43 In a BBC broadcast talk on 8 September 1964.

necessary in the Church? There is no easy answer to these questions, though it is feasible that his involvement in the Oxford heresy gave him a critical insight into the faults which had by then infiltrated Roman belief and practice.

If we accept Stevens's explanation of 'popish ditties', however, we still have to take into account the question of whether or not Taverner did continue to compose after his Oxford days.Obviously the early 1530s remain too enigmatic to support any theories on the subject, but it is difficult to believe that he did not contribute in some way to the musical life of Boston during his last eight years in the town. It is unfortunate that within a relatively well-documented period of his life there is no reference to any such activities, nor do any of his extant works point specifically to their having been written for any particular occasion during those years. From a psychological viewpoint, however, it is most unlikely that Taverner abandoned composition altogether.

Music is the composer's prime means of communication, and an essential part of himself which will break through even in the face of efforts to suppress it. It is an innate characteristic, and not a tap that can be turned on and off at will. Admittedly, extraneous circumstances can affect the style and content of a composer's output, and his total commitments obviously determine the quantity of work produced, but somehow, even in the face of opposition, a fresh idea will germinate, take shape and emerge as though it were a new life coming into the world. This in itself is reasonable cause to believe that Taverner did in fact continue to compose during his post-Oxford years, even though he might have purposely avoided writing 'popish ditties'.

PART II
HIS MUSIC

Taverner's reputation rests wholly upon a list of forty or so sacred works, all of them written for the pre-Reformation Church. This list comprises eight complete Masses along with several individual movements for the Lady Mass, eleven Votive Antiphons, three Magnificats, and settings of the Te Deum, various responds and verses, and a prose. In the secular field, one complete song and fragments of three others have survived, which, despite their relative insignificance, are worthy of more than passing mention. Although this output is not large by contemporary Netherlands standards, for example, it exceeds that of any other Tudor composer. Perhaps more important, however, is the fact that it exhibits a far wider variety of style than can be found in the work of any other English or Continental musician of the early Renaissance, thus rendering Taverner a unique and highly complex figure for study.

His extant works are to be found in about thirty manuscripts, which were copied over a period of a hundred years from the time he was at Cardinal College, and they are at present housed in the British Museum, in college libraries in Oxford, Cambridge, London and Tenbury, and in record offices in Chelmsford and Worcester.[1] About half the works appear only once in the various manuscript sources, while others exist in several copies. The *Meane Mass*, for instance, occurs in whole or in part in eight different places, the motets *Ave Dei patris filia* and *Mater Christi* in eight and ten respectively, and the large-scale Votive Antiphon *Gaude plurimum* appears in no less than nineteen manuscripts.

The fact that a work occurs in several different sources is not necessarily an indication of its popularity or of the extent to which it was originally used. Several of the manuscripts[2] that

1 The precise location of each manuscript, its reference number and Taverner content is given in the Appendix.
2 Paragraph numbers 7, 9, 10, 12, 26, 29 and 32 in the Appendix.

contain Taverner's music come from the library of Edward Paston (1550-1630) of North Norfolk, whose household maintained allegiance to Rome during the unsettled post-Henrician years. It is this private collection that accounts for seven of the nineteen extant copies of *Gaude plurimum*, and for all but one of the eight surviving manuscripts of *Sospitati dedit aegros*. Thus these two works alone owe their apparent popularity to the interests of one person. When a piece is found in several different sources, copied over a period of many years, musical and textual variations frequently occur from one manuscript to another. This is particularly so with regard to *musica ficta* and underlay, both of which were affected by changes of fashion during the course of the sixteenth and seventeenth centuries, and, in the case of *musica ficta*, by a growing predilection for major-minor tonalities which ultimately superseded the old modal system.

Many of Taverner's surviving compositions have come down to us intact, even though at times it is necessary to consult a number of manuscripts in order to build up a complete and authentic picture; but four short antiphons, *Ave Maria, Fac nobis, Sancte Deus* and *Sub tuum praesidium* each have two parts missing, and the Masses *Mater Christi* and *Small Devotion*, the *Te Deum*, the five-part *Magnificat*, and the antiphon, *Christe Jesu pastor bone* each lack a tenor part.[3]

A number of works are known to have been lost. According to a King's College Cambridge inventory of 1529, they include 'A Mass of Taverner's for Children' and some Kyries and Sequences. It is difficult to assess how many others have suffered the same fate, though it is quite possible that some of the early Marian settings could have gone astray, having been rejected on the grounds of their original associations. Other works including the *Meane Mass* and *Small Devotion*, and the Antiphons *Gaude plurimum* and *Mater Christi*[4] have survived in adaptations for use in the English Church.

A small number of pieces previously attributed to Taverner are now known to be the work of other composers. The Tudor Church Music collection contains four such pieces, namely *Tu ad liberandum* and *Tu angelorum Domina*, both identified as sections of an Antiphon by Hugh Aston, and *Rex amabilis* and *Esto nobis* from motets by Robert Fayrfax and Thomas Tallis respectively. A three-part *Osanna in excelsis* is of doubtful origin, having already been rejected as a Taverner work by the editors of the

3   In some cases reconstruction has been possible.
4   In manuscript sources 14 and 20 in the Appendix.

above-named collection, and a short Votive Antiphon, *Ave Regina Coelorum*[5], is probably spurious, being inconsistent with Taverner's style.

Before embarking upon a systematic study of Taverner's music, an explanatory note on the composer's use of voice nomenclature might be advisable, as certain terms have taken on different connotations from one century to another. His vocal parts are labelled treble, meane, countertenor, tenor and bass, the first two being boys' voices and the last three mens'. Using the Helmholz system of notation, the treble had a range of d' to g'' and the meane of g to c''. The countertenor or male alto had a range of c to g' — more in line with the tenor of today — while the Tudor tenor ranged from c to d' with occasional extensions up to e' and down to A, and the bass from F to b flat. In order to be consistent and to avoid confusion, these terms will be used in the following pages.

The Masses

Most Tudor Masses come under one of two headings, namely festal and non-festal. The festal settings were relatively long and polyphonically complex, often based upon a plainsong cantus firmus, and composed to celebrate some important feast in the church year. The non-festal were shorter, simpler in construction, and written either for the lower feast days or for general use.

Taverner's eight complete settings represent both these categories, but his crowning achievements are undoubtedly the three six-part Festal Masses, *Corona spinea*, *Gloria tibi Trinitas*, and *O Michael*. All three are preserved in the famous Forrest-Heyther part-books which date from the time when he was *Informator* at Oxford, and there is every reason to believe that these Masses were written expressly for the choir at Cardinal College. We can be almost certain that on no previous occasion would the composer have had the resources necessary to perform these works. As will be seen later, each Mass possesses individual features of interest — *Corona spinea* is the longest and most complex; *Gloria tibi Trinitas* proved to be the genesis of a large number of instrumental pieces written during the late Renaissance and early Baroque under the title of *In Nomine*; and *O Michael* explores certain experimental techniques.

Taverner's five non-festal settings show an equally varied treatment of the text, ranging from the simple dignity of the *Playn*

5 Tudor Church Music Series, (hereafter abbreviated to T.C.M.) App. 36.

Song Mass and the unusual scoring of the *Sine Nomine* or *Meane Mass*, to the more elaborate *Mater Christi, Sancti Wilhelmi* or *Small Devotion*, and the relatively complex *Western Wind* Mass.

In accordance with early Renaissance practice, Taverner's settings, both festal and non-festal, began with the *Gloria*, as the *Kyrie* was usually sung to troped plainsong. Textual cuts were also made in the *Credo*, although the sections omitted varied from one Mass setting to another. Various hypotheses have been advanced in an attempt to explain these procedures, and one writer, Ruth Hannas,[6] has suggested that the cuts in the *Credo* were determined by the then current religious or political beliefs. A simpler and perhaps more convincing explanation[7] is that a full polyphonic setting of the threefold *Kyrie* would delay for too long the opening part of the celebration of Mass. By the same token, a setting of the entire text of the *Credo*, even employing a predominantly homophonic style, would produce a disproportionately long movement. The result of these omissions, whatever the reason, together with the adoption of a more syllabic style in the still-lengthy texts of the *Gloria* and *Credo*, and a more extended melismatic treatment of the shorter texts of the *Sanctus-Benedictus* and *Agnus Dei*, created four movements of roughly equal length, which is a feature of all Taverner's settings and in fact of most Tudor Masses. This balance was often further enhanced by the use of an opening phrase or passage common to all movements, or by building the Mass on a plainsong or a secular cantus firmus.

I: THE FESTAL SETTINGS

Taverner's three Festal Masses are each based upon a plainsong melody that is broken up into separate musical phrases, sometimes ornamented with passing notes, and used throughout the four movements as a framework around which the other polyphonic parts move. Employed in this way, a cantus firmus acts as a unifying agent, which is particularly useful in long and elaborate settings. In certain cases it gives us some indication of the chronology of the work, and the purpose for which the Mass was written.

Corona spinea was probably composed to celebrate the old and now discontinued Feast of the Holy Crown of Thorns, an occasion which must have had some significance in the sixteenth century in view of the scale of Taverner's setting. It is based upon a so far

6 *Journal of the American Musicological Society*, V, pp. 155-86.
7 Denis Stevens: *Tudor Church Music*, (Faber & Faber, 1966) p. 25.

unidentified piece of plainsong which might have come from a responsory proper to the Feast, and which occurs throughout the Mass in the customary tenor voice. Although we do not know the text associated with this chant, and hence the points at which the literary phrases ended, the melody itself falls naturally into fairly clearly defined musical phrases, revealing an interesting and very satisfying structure (Ex. 1).

Ex.1

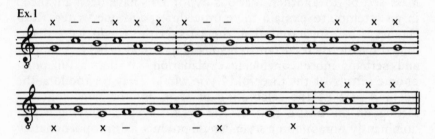

Basically it is built upon the contour of the first phrase of six notes which, expanded, produces the second phrase. The third is a decorated version of the original six notes but in inversion beginning on A, and the melody ends with an abbreviated recapitulation of the initial phrase. The whole chant therefore embodies the sonata-form principle of statement, development and restatement.

This cantus firmus appears ten times in all throughout the Mass; three times in both the *Gloria* and *Sanctus*, and twice in the *Credo* and the *Agnus Dei*. Except for one complete statement in the *Benedictus*, it is broken up into sections separated by rests, though these breaks do not always occur at the same points at each repetition of the plainsong. Furthermore, several notes of the original melody are repeated when used in the Mass. This arbitrary breaking up of a plainsong melody and the free repetition of individual notes is probably some indication that the sixteenth-century composers regarded the cantus firmus simply as scaffolding on which to build their work, and felt no necessity to retain its original structure if in that form it did not suit their purpose.

One of the major problems in composing a large-scale work such as a Festal Mass is that of producing a variety of contrasting sonorities, moods and expressions within a still-unified framework. In Tudor times this was achieved in two ways, firstly by using different groupings of voices, and secondly by varying the time signature. A combination of these two techniques was not only artistically successful, but a means of marking the progress of the Mass, and assisting in the clearer articulation of the text.

Evidence of the effectiveness of the former method can be found repeatedly throughout Taverner's music, and for an example of the antiphonal use of two groups of voices, we need look no further than the *Gloria* from *Corona spinea*[8] where the three lower parts at the words 'Tu solus Dominus' contrast with the three upper ones which reply 'Tu solus altissimus', after which they combine with all the fullness of six-part polyphony at the words 'Jesu Christe' (Ex. 2). Another example, this time of contrasting pairs of voices, occurs in the *Sanctus*[9] from the same Mass, where the countertenor and first bass sing the words 'Pleni sunt', followed by the meane and tenor who add 'coeli et terra' and the treble and second bass who complete the phrase with 'gloria tua'.

New tone-colours can also be created by the division of a voice part, a practice in which Taverner was very adept. In the *Benedictus* of *Corona spinea*, he divides his trebles at the beginning of the section 'in nomine Domini',[10] producing a gymel effect, which is joined a few bars later by the two bass parts, giving the composer the opportunity to explore the extremes of vocal range. An even more beautiful effect, resulting from the division of both trebles and meanes, is found later in the *Agnus Dei*[11] at the second occurrence of the words 'Qui tollis peccata mundi'. After a passage of exquisite four-part polyphony in the upper register, Taverner brings in the bass voice with the perfect timing and control that one associates with the oft-quoted final pedal entry in Bach's 'St Anne' Fugue for organ.

Throughout the three Festal Masses, it is noticeable that many of the transitions from one voice-grouping to another are accompanied by a change in musical style, with several passages — mostly in less than the full six parts — displaying a more elaborate melismatic treatment than the rest. This suggests that these sections of more ornate writing were possibly intended to be sung by solo voices contrasting with other passages for full choir, thus producing a quasi-concertino/ripieno effect. These 'passages of vocal music for the more expert singers', as Frank Harrison describes them,[12] provide the composer with another way of intro-

8 T.C.M. Vol. I, pp. 164-5.
9 *Ibid.*, pp. 177-9.
10 *Ibid.*, pp. 181-2.
11 *Ibid.,* pp. 188-90.
12 *Music in Medieval Britain*, 2nd ed. (Routledge & Kegan Paul), p. 262.

Ex.2 cont.

* N.B. Pause signs were used in early sixteenth-century manuscripts to indicate word settings of particular importance.

ducing variety into a large-scale choral work, as well as being useful in the enunciation of particularly poignant textual phrases. One such passage occurs in the *Credo* from *Missa Gloria tibi Trinitas* beginning at the words 'Et incarnatus est',[13] in which the melismatic writing for countertenor, tenor and bass beneath a meane cantus firmus calls for solo voices in contrast with the preceding six-part polyphony for full choir. The ornate style of this passage then contrasts still further with the next one, in which a less animated treatment emphasises the solemnity of the words 'Crucifixus etiam pro nobis'. Continued use of solo voices would be appropriate here, and variety is further obtained by the change to divided trebles, gymel-fashion, over a low bass line. This scoring then effectively prepares the way for the joyful and triumphant entry of the full choir with 'Et resurrexit'.

A closer examination of the individual movements of the Festal Masses shows that the use of different voice groupings is directly connected with the form of the works. Structurally speaking, each movement is built upon three fairly clearly defined sections of which the first and third generally contain a high proportion of six-part writing, while the middle one uses mainly smaller groups of voices. In the light of Frank Harrison's observation referred to above, the outer sections of any movement are more suited to performance by the full choir, while the inner one is in the nature of 'vocal chamber music'. Coupled with this tripartite form, as if to reinforce it, Taverner makes use of a second method by which

13 T.C.M. Vol. I, pp. 140-41.

Tudor composers introduced contrast into large-scale works, namely that of varying the time signature. It should of course be remembered that during the Renaissance this was not used to indicate accent but to show metrical relationships between notes. Throughout the Festal Masses, changes in time signature coincide with the structural divisions of a movement. In every case the movement starts off in triple measure or *tempus perfectum*, a term that has its origins in the thirteenth century and in the mediaeval concept of the Mystical Three-in-One. At the beginning of the next section there is a change to duple time, which, in many cases, is accompanied by a reduction in the number of polyphonic parts, or by a change of musical style suggesting the use of solo voices. The final section, still in duple time, is often marked by an increase in rhythmic activity, producing a drive towards the cadence.

This plan is clearly discernible in both *Corona spinea* and *O Michael*, but the use of varying time signatures is most systematically applied in *Missa Gloria tibi Trinitas*, where the mensural changes assume an important structural role. Each movement of the Mass is built upon the same plan, with the cantus firmus appearing in triple measure in the first section, in duple in the second, and in diminution of the duple in the final one. Even in the *Agnus Dei* where the cantus firmus occurs only in the outer sections of the movement, the remaining voices make the change to *tempus imperfectum* for the middle one. In this Mass, the pattern of time signature changes produces more than just contrast between sections. It also contributes in no small measure to the overall progressiveness of each movement, a need which appears to have been more acutely recognised and more systematically treated here than in any other setting.

Though marginally shorter than *Corona spinea*, *Gloria tibi Trinitas* is conceived on a similarly grand scale. By comparison it reveals an even greater mastery of construction and balance, and may justifiably be regarded as Taverner's finest work. It is named after the plainsong antiphon to the first Psalm at Lauds and Second Vespers on Trinity Sunday, and this chant provides the cantus firmus upon which the Mass is built. The work has a place of honour as the first of the original eleven settings in the Forrest-Heyther part-books, which date from the time that Taverner was at Oxford, and were probably compiled for use in Wolsey's Chapel. *Gloria tibi Trinitas* may well have been written in celebration of the First Sunday after Pentecost, a feast day which had more than its customary significance since Cardinal College was dedicated to the Holy Trinity.

The plainsong cantus firmus is used throughout the Mass, occurring three times each in the *Gloria, Credo* and *Sanctus* and twice in the *Agnus Dei*, and is given to the meane voice instead of the usual tenor. As in *Corona spinea*, it is broken up into separate phrases, except for one complete statement of the melody in the *Benedictus*, but this time the subdivisions (indicated below by bar lines) occur at the same points at each repetition of the chant (Ex. 3).

Ex.3

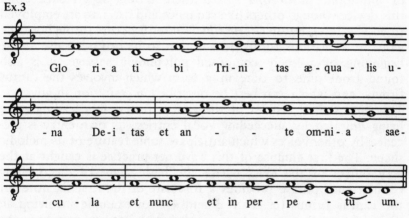

Glo - ri - a ti - bi Tri - ni - tas æ - qua - lis u -
- na De - i - tas et an - - te om - ni - a sae -
- cu - la et nunc et in per - pe - - tu - um.

(from the Sarum Antiphoner)

Sometimes the melody acquires additional passing notes, and at the beginning of the *Sanctus*[14] it appears in a varied rhythmic form within *tempus perfectum.*

An immediately noticeable feature of this Mass is that all four movements begin with what is fundamentally the same passage, which, at each repetition, varies only rhythmically in order to accommodate the different texts. This passage, scored each time for treble, meane and countertenor, extends as far as the entry of the lower voices, and consists of two subsidiary themes, which actually share a similar basic shape (Ex. 4), sung against the first three notes of the cantus firmus. Used in this way, the passage has a structural value and helps to unify the work by providing a bond between movements which, in performance, would be separated by prayers and chants proper to the day. Ex. 4 shows the subsidiary themes at their first appearance in the *Gloria.*

14 T.C.M. Vol. I, p. 145.

Ex.4

A further feature of the Mass is the regular and systematic use of imitation. In *Corona spinea* there is less dependence upon this device (though others like sequence and ostinato are employed to good effect), but in *Gloria tibi Trinitas* it occurs throughout the work in its various forms. In addition to its orthodox use at the beginning of a freely composed polyphonic passage, it is also found from time to time in a form which involves the cantus firmus, and which can best be described as imitation in advance. This means that, instead of the cantus firmus in a leading voice being imitated by succeeding vocal entries, its own entry is preceded by other voices which anticipate some feature of its melodic shape. The first glimpse of this Taverner practice is caught at the very outset of the Mass where the basic shape of the opening countertenor phrase provides a foretaste of the first six notes of the cantus firmus (cf. Exx. 3 and 4). An example involving all voices, however, occurs later in the same movement where the imitative entries at the words 'Domine Deus'[15] anticipate the third phrase of the chant which appears later at 'Rex coelestis' (Ex. 5). Treated in this way, the cantus firmus becomes an integral part of the texture, while still providing a framework upon which to build.

Another equally important form of imitation practised by Taverner is that used *within* a passage, as distinct from at its opening. This technique, which might be termed 'internal imitation', is particularly valuable in long stretches of complex polyphony, where part movement can easily become congested and the text obscured. Several examples can be found in the 'tutti' sections of *Gloria tibi Trinitas*, one of which occurs in the *Credo* beginning at the words 'et ex Patre natum'.[16] After an opening passage in free polyphony, each subsequent phrase marked by the subdivisions of the text — 'Deum de Deo', 'lumen de lumine', 'genitum non factum', 'Qui propter nos homines', etc. — is treated

15 T.C.M. Vol. I, pp. 127-8.
16 *Ibid.*, pp. 137-9.

Ex.5

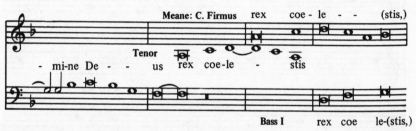

imitatively within a continuous six-part texture (Ex. 6). This enables both the literary and melodic lines to be heard more clearly, and it also assists the overall musical drive towards the cadence. Any danger of the passage sounding fragmentary is averted by the unifying presence of the cantus firmus.

A second way in which Taverner preserves the independence of the part-movement within extended tutti passages is by allowing first one voice, then another, to assume prominence within the texture. This he does by creating a more animated line for the individual voice part while simultaneously imposing restraint upon the rest. The effect of this method can be seen in the last section ('Amen') of the *Gloria* from the above Mass[17] where in a rapidly ascending scale, each voice in turn cuts through its neighbouring parts and then subsides into movement in longer note values. This enables the listener to disentangle the six-part web of sound, and follow the individual strands more easily.

On the whole, the polyphonic writing in *Gloria tibi Trinitas* is less elaborately melismatic than in *Corona spinea* where the vocal lines throughout enjoy a high degree of melodic freedom and rhythmic flexibility. Admittedly, there are several passages of a similarly florid nature in *Gloria tibi* and ample opportunity for vocal display, especially in the sections for reduced choir. Nevertheless, there is a feeling of slightly less exuberance than in *Corona*

T.C.M. Vol. I, p. 135.

Ex.6

spinea, and a tighter control of the compositional processes without the natural flow of the music being restricted. In short, the Mass demonstrates the successful wedding of technical discipline with spontaneous expression, and illustrates clearly how devices like imitation in its various forms, canon,[18] sequence,[19] and gymel[20] can still be used in a freely conceived polyphonic context without sounding laboured or contrived. Structurally, too, the Mass shows evidence of care for balance both in individual movements and in the work as a whole. Contrasting sonorities between neighbouring sections appear to have been chosen not only for their musical value, but with some consideration for the text, and each movement, especially the fine *Agnus Dei*, has a progressive quality that is an outstanding feature of this setting.

Before leaving the Mass, reference must be made to the middle section of the *Benedictus* which, detached from the rest of the

18 T.C.M. Vol. I, p. 141 ('et incarnatus est').
19 *Ibid.*, p. 152 ('Miserere nobis').
20 *Ibid.*, p. 141 ('sub Pontio Pilato' et seq.).

movement, appears in various transcriptions under the title 'In Nomine'. To quote John Caldwell,[21] this is 'a passage of singular beauty', with treble, countertenor and bass voices creating imitative arches of sounds around the meane cantus firmus, which for once is stated in a complete and unbroken form in notes of equal length and in *tempus imperfectum*. It was not uncommon for sixteenth-century composers to make favourite and outstanding passages from their large-scale works available in other arrangements, so it is no surprise to find this Taverner excerpt transcribed for keyboard in the famous Mulliner Book,[22] and in versions for solo voice with lute,[23] for viols,[24] and for four-part unaccompanied choir adapted to English words.[25]

21 *English Keyboard Music before the Nineteenth Century*, (Blackwell's Music Series) p. 73.
22 Edited by Denis Stevens, (Stainer & Bell, 1966) p. 30.
23 British Museum, MS. Add. 4900.
24 *Ibid.*, MS. Add. 31390, and Oxford: Bodleian Library Mus. Schl. MSS. d. 212-16.
25 British Museum, MSS. Add. 30480-83, and Day's *Certaine Notes* (1565).

But the matter does not end there, for works began to stream from the pens of other composers, each built upon the antiphon *Gloria tibi Trinitas* which was used as a cantus firmus as in Taverner's Mass. What is more, the form became so popular that works of this nature continued to appear in rapid succession throughout the sixteenth century and far into the seventeenth, culminating in the two fine six- and seven-part settings by Purcell. Over 150 such pieces, mainly for keyboard or instrumental ensemble, have survived in various manuscripts, and whilst some are named after the antiphon itself, most bear the title *In Nomine*.

The reason for the popularity of the antiphon has for long baffled scholars, as has the title itself, since the words 'in nomine' do not form part of the text of the original Gregorian chant, and only in recent years have answers to these questions been forthcoming.[26] It would appear that Taverner was not the only one to recognise the beauty of the aforementioned passage in his *Missa Gloria tibi Trinitas*, and the success of its transcriptions, together with the potential inherent in the cantus firmus itself, prompted other composers to write works upon the same plainsong melody. Many of these pieces bear close resemblance to the original passage in the Mass. As for the enigmatic title of these compositions, *In Nomine* is simply part of the text of the passage in Taverner's *Benedictus* that provided the initial stimulus for all later settings. It has therefore no liturgical significance as might at first be suspected, but merely acknowledges the source of inspiration for one of the most important chamber music forms of the English Renaissance.

The many outstanding qualities displayed in *Gloria tibi Trinitas*, in particular the structural balance and polyphonic fluency, are not present to the same extent in *Missa O Michael*, but considered on its own merits, this Mass is still an impressive work, and undeservedly neglected. As will be seen later, there is every indication that it was composed before the other two festal settings, but by how long it is difficult to say. The actual title *O Michael* is also difficult to explain, for instead of the Mass being based upon a plainsong of the same name, it is built upon a cantus firmus derived from part of the respond *Archangeli Michaelis interventione* (Ex. 7). This melody was the ninth respond at

26 'The Origin of the In Nomine' by Robert Donington and Thurston Dart in *Music and Letters*, Vol. XXX, No. 2 (April 1949), p. 101.
'The Origin of the English In Nomine' by Gustave Reese in the *Journal of the American Musicological Society*, Spring 1949, p. 7.

Ex.7

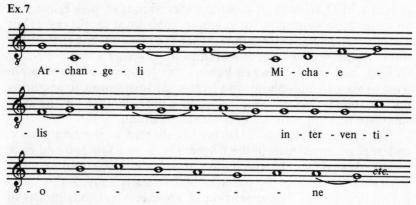

(Antiphonale Sarisburiense, Pl. 657)

Matins on the Feast of St Michael in Monte Tumba which was celebrated on 16 October, and was also sung in procession before High Mass when that date fell on a Sunday. In addition, the same plainsong was used as the third and final respond at Matins on the Feast of the Apparition of St Michael, on 8 May. Although the former of these feast days is no longer observed, it was an important occasion in the Sarum Rite, so there is good reason for suggesting that *O Michael* was written to celebrate this anniversary. The precise dating of the composition, however, presents problems, as the overall style of the piece does not correspond with the period within which such a work might have been produced and used. The immaturity of some of the part-writing and its dependence upon fifteenth-century Netherlands techniques would point to an early stage in the composer's career, yet the scale on which the Mass is written, and its association with the other settings in the Forrest-Heyther part-books, indicate that its provenance was Cardinal College. Had it been composed in Taverner's pre-Oxford days, it is unlikely that he would have had singers sufficient either in number or experience to perform the work. Certainly the choir at Tattershall with its resident six clerks and six choristers would have been inadequate to the task, and even with the additional four of each brought in to assist on high feast days, the division into six parts, and into seven for the last section of the Mass, would have been a strain on the resources. Alternatively, if one accepts the theory of a sojourn in London during the second decade of the sixteenth century, there is still no record of the composer having held an appointment that would have offered him the opportunities for performing a work of the proportions of *O Michael*. It is within the bounds of possibility that he might have written it, for example, for a royal chapel choir, but a more convincing explanation is that the Mass was the first of the three festal settings composed during Taverner's early days at Oxford, and at a time when he was still grappling with the problems of six-part polyphony and large-scale forms prior to acquiring the greater confidence expressed in *Corona spinea* or the consummate technique found in *Gloria tibi Trinitas*.

The cantus firmus in *O Michael* is allotted to the tenor voice, and appears twice each in the *Gloria*, *Credo* and *Sanctus*, and once in the *Agnus Dei*. In every case it is subdivided into sections separated by rests, or by passages of free polyphony, and it varies rhythmically from one repetition to another. Occasionally part of the plainsong melody makes a sudden transposition to the lower octave to avoid conflicting with neighbouring parts. Compared with the other two festal settings, the cantus firmus in *O Michael* is a more integral part of the overall texture, often moving in phrases that are rhythmically similar to the other five parts instead of in customary long notes. There is an attempt to create a unified structure by using a similar opening passage for the *Gloria*, *Sanctus* and *Agnus Dei*, but the practice is less consistently and less successfully applied here than in *Gloria tibi Trinitas*.

The Mass incorporates the same elements of contrast that are found elsewhere in Taverner's music, including the alternating of passages of 'vocal chamber music' with those for full choir, and the use of mensural change. There is a certain amount of congested part-writing, however, and at this stage the composer had not discovered the value of subdividing extended passages of six-part polyphony into shorter phrases, employing internal imitation. Rhythmically too, the writing is less varied than in the other two Masses, though there are signs of the composer's future ability in the bold, animated part movement at each occurrence of the words 'qui tollis peccata mundi' in the *Agnus Dei*,[27] and in the insistent use of sequence at the close of 'crucifixus etiam' from the *Credo*.[28] A prominent feature of the work is Taverner's use of canon, which in each case possesses a natural flow without any feeling of it having been forced. Canons appear in all four movements of *O Michael*. Notable amongst these is a two-in-one at the unison for divided trebles over a free bass part at 'Qui tollis' from the *Gloria*,[29] and a more elaborate similarly-scored one at

27 T.C.M. Vol. I, pp. 219-20 and 221-2.
28 *Ibid.*, p. 208.
29 *Ibid.*, pp. 199-200.

the beginning of the *Benedictus*.[30] A two-in-one at the second for divided trebles against a free meane part occurs at 'Filium Dei unigenitum' in the *Credo*,[31] and a very effective one at the unison for two basses beneath a pair of independent upper voices can be found at the third 'Agnus Dei'[32] (Ex. 8).

Viewing the setting as a whole, there is evidence of an increased confidence in the part writing as the work proceeds, culminating in an audacious piece of seven-part polyphony for the closing phrase, 'Dona nobis pacem'.[33] This is the only occasion when Taverner writes for this number of voices, and although the texture is a little turgid in places, the divided basses provide a continuous and solid foundation for the upper voices so that the two together add up to a very sonorous coda.

II: THE NON-FESTAL SETTINGS

The best known and most widely performed work by Taverner is the *Western Wind* Mass. This is one of the five non-festal settings, but differs from its companions in having a certain affinity with the festal variety. Although it is shorter than the three six-part works already discussed and is scored for only four voices, it incorporates a great deal of florid polyphonic writing, particularly in the third and fourth movements, and at times displays an element of exuberance reminiscent of *Corona spinea*. It has a unique place both in Taverner's output and on a wider plane, as it is the first known English Mass to be built upon a secular cantus firmus. For many years it had been common practice for Continental composers to base their works upon folk tunes, chansons and the like — *L'homme armé* and *Se la face ay pale* spring immediately to mind — but in this country only plainsong melodies had so far been used.

Many questions still surround the *Western Wind*, and there continues to be disagreement over its date of origin and the purpose for which it was composed. Even the cantus firmus poses problems as its melodic shape differs substantially from the courtly song upon which the Mass is supposedly based. Nevertheless, Taverner's setting in both its complete sources[34] carries the same title as the song. The only link that can at present be found

30 T.C.M. Vol. I, p. 216.
31 *Ibid*., p. 204.
32 *Ibid*., pp. 222-3.
33 *Ibid*., pp. 224-5.
34 Appendix, paragraphs 4 and 15.

Ex.8

between this song and the cantus firmus of the Mass has to be traced through the contents of two manuscripts that were possibly compiled during the years 1515 to 1520 for use at Court, and are now preserved in the British Museum as Royal Appendix Numbers 56 and 58.

The second of these began life as a part book containing about twenty courtly songs to which were later added the tenor lines from various sacred works, and over thirty instrumental pieces, some of which had close associations with the Monarch such as the *King Harry VIIIth Pavan*. One of the original songs was a monophonic setting in transposed Hypodorian Mode of a single verse beginning 'Westron Wynd, when wyll thow blow' (Ex. 9).

Ex. 9

Wes - tron wynd, when wyll - - thow blow. The

smalle rayne downe can rayne? Cryst yf my love were in my armys and

I yn my bed a - gayne.

(transcribed in quarter note values)

Aesthetically this melody has a most attractive curve, and is structurally well balanced despite its phrases of varying length. Stylistically it is typical of the courtly songs of the day, and bears a close resemblance, particularly in the opening line and in the cadential flourish, to the melody of Henry VIII's own *Pastime with Good Company*. One is tempted to suggest that the King might have been influenced by the song, or even based his own work upon it, an accepted practice of the time. Be that as it may, on first acquaintance it does not appear that Taverner based *his* work on the same song, for, from its very outset, the cantus firmus of the *Western Wind* Mass pursues a different melodic line (Ex. 10).

Closer examination of the two tunes, however, reveals certain features common to both, including the style and some of the rhythmic figuration. The first phrase of each tune is also basically the same (as is shown by the asterisks and brackets in the above

Ex.10

(note values quartered to correspond with Ex. 9)

quotations), and the third phrase, B² of Ex. 10, is an elongated and modified version of the last two and a half bars of the original song.

The two tunes are therefore more closely related than they at first appear to be, and there is a possibility that the cantus firmus developed out of the courtly song. If this were so, it is more likely the result of a conscious effort on the part of Taverner than from any natural development through repeated performance. There are certain factors supporting this suggestion, the first being that the cantus firmus form of the melody has the mark of a professional composer about it. It is more formal in design than the song tune, and is built on three phrases of similar length, the third a variation of the second, giving an overall plan of A, B¹, B². It is also more suited to polyphonic treatment, especially in its initial rising fifth and the relative simplicity of the penultimate bar, and it points to having been constructed with this idea in mind.

If the above argument is not in itself sufficiently convincing, the link between the two tunes is strengthened by reference to the other of the two manuscripts, Royal Appendix 56, which appears to be a companion to Number 58 as the paper in each case carries the same watermark. Number 56 is another miscellaneous collection of songs and instrumental pieces[35], including further polyphonic parts to six of the compositions contained in Manuscript 58. The most interesting item at this juncture, however, is a brief excerpt from the opening of the *Agnus Dei* from Taverner's *Western Wind* Mass showing the treble and tenor voices only, arranged in keyboard format. The cantus firmus does not appear as it lies in the bass at this point in the full score. Although the

35 Appendix, paragraph 1.

presence of this quotation does not provide any proof of a connection between the Mass and the courtly song, it adds feasibility to this line of thought, and it also points to the *Western Wind* being a product of the composer's early years. Furthermore, if this composer were the Taverner of the St Nicholas Bede Roll, the work might conceivably date from the second decade of the sixteenth century, and so precede the settings built on the same cantus firmus by Christopher Tye (c.1500-75) and John Shepherd (c.1520-63). It would also seem logical that Taverner's only Mass to be based upon a secular tune should originate at a time and place when he was perhaps most aware of the courtly songs of the Henrician household, and at the point when his own settings of love lyrics (q.v.) were probably composed.

Whatever date we provisionally attach to the *Western Wind* Mass, however, there still remains the question of the purpose for which it was written. Various theories have been advanced, including a suggestion that the work was an offering made by Taverner in the hope of securing an appointment at Court; but until more information comes to hand, one can only continue to indulge in speculation. Meanwhile, the two complete extant copies of the Mass show it to be a highly organised piece of composition.

The song tune used in the *Western Wind* (Ex. 10) is not employed in the same way as the cantus firmus in the festal settings. Instead it is repeated thirty-six times in all throughout the Mass, nine times in each movement, and forms the basis of a series of polyphonic variations. There is no attempt to disguise its secular origins by burying it in an inner part, for it is given to the trebles no less than twenty-one times. Elsewhere it appears in the countertenor, and occasionally in the bass. The repetitions of the melody are continuous throughout the work, and there are no breaks between one statement and the next, even when it transfers from one voice to another. The corresponding note values remain fairly constant at each repetition of the tune, though from time to time the cadence is decorated with passing notes and auxiliary notes. Once in each movement the third phrase of the melody (B^2 in Ex. 10) is omitted, and in the final statement in the *Gloria, Credo* and *Agnus Dei*, the theme goes into compound time.

One of the most notable features of the Mass is its form, and although this is primarily determined by the repetitions of the basic song tune, there is also evidence of further careful planning by the composer. The *Gloria* and *Credo* are both built upon the same pattern, and there are structural relationships between the *Sanctus* and *Agnus Dei*. In the former case, both movements subdivide into two large sections, A and B, each comprising four statements of the basic melody followed by a coda on the ninth repetition in compound time. Internal balance is then created in each movement where three statements of the melody in section A occur in 'tutti' passages and the other in a passage for reduced choir, while in section B the opposite applies, with one statement for full choir and three for reduced choir. The coda is also for full choir.

In the *Sanctus* and *Agnus Dei*, balance derives from a more subtle scheme of working. Here both movements subdivide into three large sections, A, B, and C, each with three statements of the basic melody. One analysis shows section A of both movements to be built upon the same plan, with two statements of the tune in full choir passages and the other in duo or trio. After this, the two sections B and C of the *Sanctus* balance, each with one statement for full choir and two for reduced choir, while in the *Agnus Dei*, section B is scored entirely for two or three voices, which balances and also contrasts with section C for full choir throughout. A second and broader analysis of the two movements shows the *Sanctus* with four full-choir and five reduced-choir statements of the basic melody, balancing five for full choir and four for reduced choir in the *Agnus Dei*.

It is of course possible to read far more into structural design than perhaps the composer ever envisaged, but from the foregoing observations alone, it is obvious that the *Western Wind* Mass is the result of some very systematic planning. Furthermore, the confidence shown in its construction points to it being a more mature work than manuscript evidence might at first indicate. This view could also be extended to the part writing itself which reveals a considerable variety of melodic and rhythmic invention. The *Agnus Dei*, for example, contains some effective use of triplet figuration such as that in the countertenor line at the words 'peccata mundi'[36] (Ex. 11). Tonal contrast, too, is always present, both in the scoring for full and reduced choir, and also between the predominantly syllabic style of the four-part writing and the often florid duo and trio passages.

Imitation is found throughout the Mass, though it is generally not carried beyond the initial two or three notes, and the internal form of this device is not a feature of the writing. Neither is canon, but from time to time, the repetition of a short phrase

36 T.C.M. Vol. I, p. 23.

Ex.11

such as that which occurs in the countertenor at '(Domine) Deus, Agnus Dei' in the *Gloria*[37] helps to unify a passage.

Stylistically the *Western Wind* has a foot in both the festal and non-festal camps, but the remaining four Taverner Masses are conceived on relatively simple lines. Some contain extended passages of homophony in which syllabic word setting is predominant. Elsewhere the writing is florid, and at times highly ornate, but there is a certain restraint both in phrase-length and pitch-range compared with those works already discussed. Nevertheless there is still much of interest, and between themselves the four Masses vary considerably in length, construction and vocal scoring. The cantus firmus principle is not used in any of them; but two, namely *Mater Christi* and *Sancti Wilhelmi* or *Small Devotion*, fall into the category of the parody-mass.

The term 'parody' refers to the fifteenth- and sixteenth-century practice of building a work upon the musical material of another pre-existing one. Examples of Masses based upon melodies or

37 T.C.M. Vol. I, p. 5.

complete polyphonic passages drawn from chansons and motets are common in the work of Continental composers, but relatively rare in this country. In fact, apart from the tentative use which Robert Fayrfax makes of a vocal line from an antiphon in the composition of his Mass *O bone Jesu*,[38] Taverner appears to be the first English composer to employ parody-techniques systematically.

The Mass *Mater Christi* is named after the short Votive Antiphon upon which it is based. The sole manuscript source of the Mass is the 'Henrician' part books[39] of which the tenor is missing. In view of the extent to which the parody principle is applied, however, a considerable amount of reconstruction has been possible[40] by using the Antiphon *Mater Christi*, which has survived intact in the 'Sadler' part books as well as in incomplete form in several other manuscripts.

In the composition of the Mass, Taverner took the opening and closing passages of the original Antiphon and adapted them for use as the first and last sections of each of the four movements. In some cases the transfer involved little more than substituting a new text, *contrafactum* fashion, whilst in others it meant changing note values and rhythmic stress in order to accommodate different words. Sometimes the polyphonic parts acquired a few decorative passing-notes in the course of transfer. All these features can be seen by comparing the initial passages of the Antiphon and the *Gloria* of the Mass (Ex. 12). The scoring in each case is for treble and meane.

Passages from the middle of the motet are also used in the course of the Mass, but here the part writing has often undergone major change, and at times only the general outline of the original quotation is retained. The remaining portions of the Mass that are not derived from the Antiphon consist of new music composed for the purpose.

In spite of the interest created by the use of parody-techniques, however, *Mater Christi* does not live up to its initial promise. The quotations from the Antiphon do not seem to be successfully integrated with the new material, so that structurally the work lacks continuity, and the musical ideas are somewhat dissipated. This impression may be due partly to the fact that the original Antiphon is recognisable in a fragmentary form in the Mass, for

38 British Museum: Harley Manuscript 1709, f. 53.
39 Appendix, paragraph 21.
40 By the Editors of *Tudor Church Music*, Intro. pp. lxi-lxii and pp. 99ff.

Ex.12

there is no appreciable reworking of the parodied passages, and therefore no fresh interest is kindled. It might almost be said that the Antiphon loses certain of its qualities rather than gains in stature by the transfer of material.

There are nevertheless some compensating features in the part-writing, including imitation and canonic treatment, sequence and ostinato. Imitation did not play a significant part in the work of fiteenth-century English composers, although it had long been an important device on the Continent, but it began to make regular appearances in the music of Taverner. In *Mater Christi* it is extensively and effectively used, often in a very close form, for example in the *Sanctus* beginning at the words 'Dominus Deus'.[41] At times the imitation is carried some distance, and provides a certain thrust to the polyphonic writing as in the four-part final 'Agnus Dei'[42] (Ex. 13).

Elsewhere it becomes a near canon, as in the two-part passage at the second occurrence of the same words.[43]

41 T.C.M. Vol. I, pp. 114-15.
42 *Ibid.*, p. 124.
43 *Ibid.*, p. 122.

Ex.13

(N.B. Tenor voice is missing)

In contrast with these polyphonic passages, sections in homophonic style are common throughout the work, and often involve the antiphonal use of upper and lower voices. This style and treatment is usually applied by Renaissance composers to settings of long texts like the *Gloria* and *Credo*, in which the end of a phrase sung by one group of voices is allowed to overlap the beginning of the next one sung by another group. In *Mater Christi*, this method is found in the common opening to each of the four movements. It is also found in the *Credo* at the words 'et iterum venturus est',[44] which shows the division of the full five-part texture into a treble-meane 'choir' alternating with, and overlapping, another 'choir' of countertenor, tenor and bass.

Another parody Mass by Taverner is often referred to as *Small Devotion*. Its title in the manuscript sources[45] is difficult to decipher, and this curious name is the Tudor Church Music Editors' interpretation, and is not altogether convincing. Another interpretation, based upon a very reasoned and scholarly argument by Denis Stevens,[46] is that the original title was *Sancti Wilhelmi Devotio* which, in the course of time and in the hands of various copyists, became abbreviated to *S. Will. Devotio*, and so corrupted to *Small Devotion*. The St William in the title is the twelfth-century Archbishop of York, whose memory was honoured in one of the three antiphons sung daily after Compline in Thomas Wolsey's College at Oxford.[47] The Mass is built to a certain extent upon

44 T.C.M. Vol. I, p. 111.
45 Appendix, paragraphs 14, 21, 25 and 28.
46 Stevens: *Tudor Church Music*, 2nd Edn. (Faber) p. 33, and *Die Musik in Geschichte und Gegenwart*, Vol. XIII, 1949, 68. Also Harrison: *Music and Letters*, XLVI, 1965, p. 382.
47 J. H. Parker: *The Statutes of the Colleges of Oxford*, Vol. II.

Taverner's Antiphon *Christe Jesu pastor bone*, a worк which Stevens suggests might formerly have carried a different text, associated with St William. The connection between the Saint and the Antiphon, and between the Antiphon and the Mass, adds weight to a theory that the setting might have been composed to celebrate the tercentenary of the canonisation of William of York which took place on 21 March 1526, a few months after Taverner's arrival at Cardinal College.

Looking beyond the questions of title and purpose, however, *Missa Sancti Wilhelmi* or *Small Devotion* is musically more attractive and structurally more integrated than the previously discussed *Mater Christi*. In common with that setting, it has come down to us without its tenor part, but this time any reconstruction by way of the parent antiphon is impossible, as it too lacks the same voice-part in both its manuscript sources.[48] Compared with *Mater Christi, Sancti Wilhelmi* relies very little upon parody-techniques. Certain sections of the work are derived from either the opening or closing passages of *Christe Jesu*, but for the most part the Mass consists of newly-composed material. The first case of borrowing comes at the very beginning of the *Gloria*[49] where the opening section is built upon a varied version of the initial two phrases of the Antiphon. These same two phrases are also used in the *Agnus Dei*, not, as one would expect, at the beginning of the movement, but at the first 'miserere nobis'.[50] A further quotation from the early part of the Antiphon[51] occurs again in the *Gloria* at the words 'Domine fili unigenite'.[52] The closing passages of both the *Gloria*[53] and *Agnus Dei*[54] are also derived from *Christe Jesu*, this time from its final phrase, sung originally to the words 'aeternae vitae premio'. Beyond these direct borrowings, occasional passing references to the Antiphon are found in the Mass, but more in the spirit than in the letter.

Thus, *Christe Jesu* played a very small part in the composition of *Sancti Wilhelmi*, and was not even used to provide a common opening to each of the four movements as in the case of *Mater Christi*. Nevertheless, the work is a coherent structure and contains a great deal of mature part-writing which, in the latter half of the Mass, approaches a festal style. At times there are passages of

48 Appendix, paragraphs 18 and 21.
49 T.C.M. Vol. I, p. 70.
50 *Ibid.*, p. 94.
51 Originally set to 'Cleri fautor'.
52 T.C.M. Vol. I, p. 71.
53 *Ibid.*, p. 76.
54 *Ibid.*, p. 98.

outstanding beauty like the 'Osanna' in the *Sanctus*[55] (Ex. 14), with its rising sequential countertenor phrase acting as a unifying element, and producing a driving force that carries the music right through to the final cadence.

Technically speaking, imitation is regularly used in the *Sanctus* and *Agnus Dei*, and sometimes provides a clue as to how the missing tenor line might have read.[56] The antiphonal use of upper and lower voices also occurs frequently, creating contrasting sonorities. Mensural change is another feature of the Mass, each movement starting off in *tempus perfectum* and giving way to duple measure in the coda. All this adds up to a work of some distinction, and its various characteristics and attributes tend to support the theory that *Missa Sancti Wilhelmi* might well be a product of the composer's Oxford years.

The remaining two Masses by Taverner command immediate attention by reason of their unusual scoring. One of them, the five-part *Meane Mass*, is so called because it dispenses with treble voices, leaving as the uppermost line a high meane part with a range c' to c''. It is also known as *Sine Nomine*, a title used to denote a Mass composed upon original material as distinct from one built on a cantus firmus. It is the shortest of the eight complete settings, and, from a study of its stylistic features, possibly post-dates the others. Structurally it is bound together by opening and closing passages common to all four movements, a technique already found in *Mater Christi*. A feature of even greater interest, however, is the consistency in the style of writing used throughout the Mass. Although somewhat restrained when compared with the festal settings or the *Western Wind*, there is a refined quality about the polyphony, and the individual parts trace smooth, graceful curves of predominantly conjunct movement. Contrast is still a feature, but it depends more upon regular mensural change than upon the varied scoring of adjacent passages.

Compared with the works discussed so far, the *Meane Mass* shows a high regard for both musical and textual clarity, and a greater awareness of the need for appropriate word setting. Its success in these respects stems largely from the habitual use of imitation which occurs in various forms throughout the Mass. One variety that has not hitherto been prominent in Taverner's

55 T.C.M. Vol. I, p. 89.
56 See for example the phrases beginning 'Pleni sunt' in the *Sanctus* (T.C.M. Vol. I, p. 87) and 'qui tollis' in the *Agnus Dei*, (*Ibid.*, p. 93), and the way in which the Editors of T.C.M. have supplied the missing part.

Ex.14

Text: "Osanna in excelsis"

writing is imitation by pairs of voices. Two examples can be found in the *Gloria*. The first is at 'suscipe deprecationem'[57] where the two-part counterpoint in the tenor and bass is imitated by the meane and countertenor respectively, entering later as a pair. The second is at 'Quoniam tu solus'[58] where the two lower parts are likewise imitated by the upper two (Ex. 15). In the *Credo*, at the

Ex.15

words 'Crucifixus etiam',[59] the antecedent meane and counter-tenor phrase is subsequently taken up by the tenor and bass. This pairing of entries for imitative purposes is characteristic of the fifteenth-century Netherlands School, but it did not constitute part of the technique of English composers until mid-Tudor times. With this in mind, we have one good reason for regarding the Meane Mass as a product of Taverner's latter years.

Another feature supporting the late dating of the work is the regular occurrence of a type of imitation previously described as 'internal' and associated with the composer's mature style of writing. Effective examples of this have already been noticed in discussing *Missa Gloria tibi Trinitas*.[60] Its use in the *Meane Mass* bears the hallmark of the experienced artist, as is shown by examining the long section from the *Credo* beginning with the words 'passus et sepultus est' and extending as far as 'ad dexteram patris'.[61] In the course of this section Taverner constructs his

57 T.C.M. Vol. I, p. 53.
58 *Ibid.*, p. 54.
59 *Ibid.*, p. 58.
60 See page 48.
61 T.C.M. Vol. I, pp. 58-60.

voice parts not as long, unbroken rhapsodic lines of counterpoint but from short, rhythmic phrases, separated by rests, which are then treated imitatively, either individually or in pairs. Employed in this way, imitation begins to play a primary role in the structural scheme of the work, as well as contributing to musical and textual clarity.

In his attempts to achieve a more direct mode of expression and an articulate rendering of the words, Taverner does not simply resort to extended passages in homophonic style. Instead he creates a mainly polyphonic texture throughout the Mass, but one in which the individual lines are separated into clear-cut phrases with short melismas on important words, and syllabic treatment elsewhere. This even applies to the more ornate *Sanctus* and *Agnus Dei*. In addition several passages, especially in the *Gloria* and *Credo*, involve the repetition of textual phrases, a feature not so far discovered in the earlier works of this composer.

In the light of all these observations, the *Meane Mass* shows itself to be very close to the principles and practice of the late Renaissance, and one can therefore appreciate the significance of a statement made by Hugh Benham[62] that in this setting 'we can see, more clearly perhaps than anywhere else, those aspects of Taverner's technique which were to influence later English composers'.

Finally we come to the *Playn Song Mass* which is a most austere setting and unique in Taverner's output. It is scored for mens' voices only, in a mainly continuous four-part texture, and has survived in a single manuscript source known as the 'Gyffard' part-books[63] which were probably copied during the reign of Queen Mary.[64] The origin of the title is rather puzzling as no plainsong melody has been used in the construction of the Mass, but it has been suggested that it derives from the very limited number of note values found in the work, namely the breve and semibreve, and, in company with a dotted semibreve, the occasional minim.

It is also difficult to find a reason for its composition, though it could have been written late in Taverner's career as a reaction against his earlier florid settings of the Mass, and those of his contemporaries. We know that, during the mid-sixteenth century,

62 In a broadcast talk on BBC Radio 3, 21 August 1971.
63 Appendix, paragraph 4.
64 Harrison: *Music in Medieval Britain*, (Routledge & Kegan Paul), pp. 288-9.

works of a highly ornate character came under attack from Thomas Cranmer and other writers of the day, who were advocating simpler forms of service in which words were not obscured by elaborate polyphony.[65] It is possible that Taverner in his later years also subscribed to these same views, which would be consistent with his efforts in Boston and elsewhere to rid the Church of its extraneous trappings. If this argument supports the theory of a late dating of the work, however, its style fails to do so, for it incorporates techniques that belong to a much earlier period of composition, and does not carry the stamp of the mature artist as did the *Meane Mass*. It follows, therefore, that until fresh evidence comes to hand, the purpose for which the piece was written and its date of origin must remain open questions.

Although there is a vague similarity between the initial phrases of the four movements of the *Playn Song Mass*, no conscious effort appears to have been made to link them through a common opening passage as in *Mater Christi* or the *Meane Mass*. Structurally the first two movements are built upon a sequence of adjacent phrases employing contrasting styles and techniques. For example, the *Credo*[66] starts out with 'Patrem omnipotentem' in simple polyphony, followed by 'factorem coeli et terra' in homophonic style. Polyphony then resumes at 'visibilium', after which 'Et in unum Dominum' is given chordal treatment. The next phrase, 'filium Dei', employs simple imitation, followed by more homophony at 'et ex Patre'.

Throughout the *Gloria* and *Credo* the voices proceed in a predominantly syllabic style (Ex. 16). Conjunct movement is a prominent feature, and phrases are built upon a narrow range of notes. The *Sanctus* and *Agnus Dei*, however, present a rather different picture. Here a more polyphonic style is used, with many long rhapsodic phrases sung to single syllables, and a marked absence of punctuating rests. Imitation often occurs at the beginning of a section, but the internal variety — such an asset in achieving textual clarity — is hardly ever found. Conjunct movement is still much in evidence but it is now in company with sizeable melodic leaps, and phrases often employ a wider pitch range than in earlier movements.

There are several noteworthy passages in the *Playn Song Mass*, and the *Gloria* and *Credo* in particular possess a dignity all of their own. But the work as a whole is uneven, inconsistent in style, and employs archaic techniques. There is an obvious attempt in the

65 Peter le Huray: *Music and the Reformation in England* (1967).
66 T.C.M. Vol. I, pp. 34ff.

Ex.16

first two movements to create a simple and direct form of expression, and one that would correspond with the supposed views of the composer during his later years, but it is difficult to understand why he should have found it necessary to adopt outdated practices in the remainder of the work. One might even be tempted to suggest that the two halves of the Mass were written at different times during Taverner's career, for so hybrid a setting can hardly be regarded in toto as a product of his artistic maturity.

III: MISCELLANEOUS MOVEMENTS FOR THE LADY MASS

In addition to the eight complete Masses, a number of separate movements by Taverner have been preserved, mainly in single manuscript sources, comprising a four-part *Kyrie* known as 'Leroy', three different settings of *Christe eleison* and two *Alleluias*. Each of these compositions was originally part of a setting for the Lady Mass, which in small churches was celebrated once a week, and in large establishments daily throughout the year. For this second purpose complete cycles of seven Masses, one for each day of the week, were composed, though only one such cycle by Nicholas Ludford[67] (c.1480-c.1542) has survived intact. It is not known if the Taverner works just mentioned were initially part of complete cycles, but it is a possibility, and in view of their Marian associations they could all date from the composer's Oxford years.

The *Kyrie* and *Christe* settings are built upon cantus firmi which are derived from a fifteenth-century collection of non-liturgical melodies known as squares. These melodies became stock-in-trade material for the composition of Lady Masses, a practice that continued until the mid-sixteenth century. The tunes used by Taverner are also found in the Ludford cycle, whose part-books indicate that in certain of the Masses the *Kyrie* and parts of the *Gloria* and *Credo* were performed *alternatim*.[68] This means that the text was sung in alternation, first by a solo voice to the basic melody or square itself, and then by the choir in the polyphonic setting built upon that square. From this we can deduce that the Taverner works were no doubt treated in the same way.

The sole manuscript source of *Kyrie Leroy* is the 'Gyffard' part-books[69] which possibly date from the third quarter of the sixteenth century. The title 'Leroy' is the name given to the square for the Sunday Lady Mass upon which the *Kyrie* is built (Ex. 17).[70] Used as a cantus firmus, this melody is given to the treble voice where it is ornamented with additional passing-notes. The texture is florid throughout, with long rhapsodic phrases sung to single syllables. Imitation is almost totally absent, but there is no danger of words being lost in so short and familiar a text. Although the writing does not represent Taverner's most mature style, there is much to admire. The continuous four-part polyphony is remarkably transparent, and within the work's brief span there is considerable rhythmic variety. The third section (Kyrie) begins with a mensural change from compound to simple time, and a gradual shortening of note-values produces a convincing drive to the cadence.

The three short settings of *Christe eleison* are based upon the second section of the square for the Tuesday Lady Mass (Ex. 18). In the first two settings it appears in the middle voice and in the third it is given to the trebles. In each case, the other two voices

67 British Museum: Royal Appendix 45-8.
68 *New Oxford History of Music*, Vol. III, pp. 335-6.
69 Appendix, paragraph 4.
70 The fifteen squares together with an article on the subject by Hugh Baillie are printed in *Acta Musicologica*, 1960 (Bärenreiter), p. 188.

Ex.17

Ex.18

sing florid, independent lines against the cantus firmus, with one imitative entry occurring at the beginning of the second *Christe*. Again the texture is transparent, but the settings are un-distinguished.

Alleluia Salve virgo and *Alleluia Veni electa mea* [71] were also written for the Lady Mass, and are in each case four-part poly-phonic settings of the choral part of the respond. Before Taverner's time it was general practice for the opening of the respond and its verse to be sung in polyphony and the choral parts in plainsong, but in the early sixteenth century the reverse procedure began to find favour. Thus in performance each of the above settings would

71 Entitled *Alleluia* I and II respectively in T.C.M. Vol. III, pp. 52 and 53.

be preceded by the word 'Alleluia' sung by the soloist to plainchant, and would be followed by the verse, the first half sung by
the soloist again to plainchant, and the second half by the choir
using the same music as that of the polyphonic 'Alleluia'. The
whole would then be rounded off with a final 'Alleluia' sung to
plainchant by the soloist as in the opening section of the respond,
but omitting any *jubilus* which might initially have been present.

Both *Alleluias* have survived in the 'Gyffard' part-books,[72] the
source of so many Taverner works, though a version of the second
one also occurs in a later manuscript collection of songs with lute
accompaniment.[73] The works are each built upon a cantus firmus,
but the origin of the one used in the first *Alleluia* is not clear. It
is given to the tenor voice, and, according to Frank Harrison,[74]
resembles the melodies of both *Salve virgo* and *Virga Jesse floruit*
used respectively at the Friday and Saturday Lady Masses. Beyond
this general resemblance, however, certain passages of the cantus
firmus are identical with passages in both chants.[75] Since the two
melodies are quite independent of each other, there seems to be
no logical reason for combining them to produce a cantus firmus,
and one is left with the possibility of the *Alleluia* being built upon
a so far unidentified chant. Meanwhile Harrison refers to the work
as *Salve virgo*, a title that appears to be generally accepted. The
second *Alleluia* presents no such problems for it is based upon the
melody *Veni electa mea* of the Thursday Lady Mass, which is
transposed a perfect fourth higher and placed in the treble.

Like *Kyrie Leroy*, both *Alleluias* are written in florid style, but
here there is also evidence of approaching maturity. The first
one begins with a hint of imitation by pairs of voices, after which
the long melismatic lines are broken up into concise, manageable
phrases separated by rests, creating a lucid texture and allowing
the music to 'breathe'. Several of the phrases begin imitatively
and follow the same descending scalic pattern. The second
Alleluia opens canonically, with tenor and bass voices anticipating
the cantus firmus in the treble (Ex. 19). After this, the gradual
introduction of shorter note-values urges the music forward
towards the animated scale passages of the closing bars.

Finally, the Tudor Church Music Series included fragments of a
three-part *Agnus Dei* which is found in company with a number of

72 Appendix, paragraph 4.
73 *Ibid.*, paragraph 5.
74 *Music in Medieval Britain*, (Routledge & Kegan Paul), p. 292.
75 Found in the Sarum Graduals of 1507 and 1532.

Ex.19

other Taverner works in a single manuscript source of the late sixteenth or early seventeenth century.[76] It is built out of gracefully shaped phrases in which conjunct movement is predominant, and strict imitation a regular feature, but some scholars doubt its authenticity on stylistic grounds.

The Antiphons

The second field in which Taverner made a marked and valuable contribution was that of the Votive Antiphon. Works of this description were widely used during the Renaissance, and consisted of verse or prose settings, liturgical or otherwise, sung during devotions which followed evening Compline. The words would often be of a petitionary nature, general or specific in content, and, in the majority of cases, expressed in the name of the Blessed Virgin Mary. The most comprehensive source of English Marian Antiphons is the famous Eton Choir Book[77] which originally contained sixty-seven such works dating from the second half of the fifteenth century.

In common with the Mass settings, antiphons varied considerably in length, structure and style. Some were large-scale works of polyphonic complexity, composed for use on high feast days or in commemoration of some important figure or event, whilst others were conceived on more modest lines, often in less ornate counterpoint, to serve daily observance. This variety is clearly illustrated in Taverner's eleven antiphons, which comprise three large-scale festal settings, *Ave Dei patris filia*, *Gaude plurimum*, and *O splendor gloriae*; six short ones, *Ave Maria, Mater Christi, Sub tuum praesidium, Christe Jesu pastor bone, Fac nobis* and *Sancte Deus* — the first three Marian and the second three

76 Appendix, paragraph 12.
77 Eton College MS. 178.

in the Name of Jesus; and two further settings, *Prudens Virgo* and *Virgo pura*, which are probably excerpts from larger works.

On first acquaintance with the large-scale Antiphons one might be tempted to seek parallels between them and the three Festal Masses, and thereby discover their date of origin and the purpose for which they were composed. In view of their length and complexity one may safely assume that they were written for more than routine use and for an experienced choir, and Cardinal College immediately springs to mind as a likely provenance. In the case of *Ave Dei patris filia* and *Gaude plurimum*, however, source material soon disposes of this line of thought since both works are found in two manuscripts dating from about 1520[78] and compiled for use at the Chapel Royal. In one of them,[79] of which only the meane part-book has survived, the Antiphons are both unattributed, though *Gaude plurimum* is given pride of place as the first work in the collection. It is possible, therefore, that both pieces were products of the second decade of the sixteenth century, and roughly contemporary with the *Western Wind* Mass. If this were so, we are still no nearer to the purpose for which the works were written, but their presence in the aforementioned manuscripts at least lends support to the theory that Taverner spent some time in London during his early career.

The earliest surviving manuscript sources of the third Antiphon, *O splendor gloriae*, are those compiled by John Baldwin[80] and John Sadler[81] dated 1581 and 1585 respectively. In each case it is found together with *Ave Dei patris filia* and *Gaude plurimum*, though the Sadler is the only complete source as the tenor part-book is missing from the other set. In Baldwin's manuscript, the Antiphon is attributed to Taverner and Tye, the latter having supposedly completed the work by adding the section beginning 'Et cum pro nobis'.[82] Although some writers[83] have accepted this joint authorship, it is questionable on two counts at least; firstly because Sadler, who has proved to be a more reliable informant than Baldwin, attributes the piece in its entirety to Taverner, and secondly because the writing is stylistically consistent throughout. The reason for its composition is not clear, but as it is a Trinity Antiphon, there is a possibility that it might have been written

78 Appendix, paragraphs 2, 23 and 24.
79 *Ibid.*, paragraph 2, known as the Harleian Manuscript.
80 *Ibid.*, paragraph 18.
81 *Ibid.*, paragraph 15.
82 T.C.M. Vol. III, p. 103.
83 Including H. B. Collins: *Music and Letters*, VI, p. 315.

for use at Cardinal College, which was dedicated to the Holy Trinity, St Frideswide and All Saints. It is perhaps too substantial a setting for the regular observances set forth in the college statutes,[84] and some high feast day such as Trinity Sunday would have been a more appropriate occasion on which to use it. Without pursuing these theories any further, however, we can be fairly certain that, on stylistic grounds alone, *O Splendor gloriae* post-dates the other two large-scale Antiphons.

All three works are polyphonically complex, but by comparison, *Ave Dei patris filia* is the most florid, and its independent voice parts and melismatic word settings are strongly reminiscent of *Missa Corona spinea*. It is also the longest of the three Antiphons. The origin of the text is as yet unknown, but its seven concise and balanced verses in honour of the Blessed Virgin Mary appealed to a number of Tudor composers including Fayrfax and Tallis, both of whom produced a five-part setting.[85] The use of a cantus firmus in an early sixteenth-century Votive Antiphon is very unusual, but Taverner has built his *Ave Dei* upon the *Te Deum* chant which is given to the tenor voice in long note-values.

The piece has considerable tonal variety, and, although it is continuous throughout, a fresh vocal scoring coincides with the beginning of each stanza of the text. In common with the Festal Masses, there are passages for full choir and others for reduced forces. Noteworthy amongst the latter are two sonorous sections for countertenor, tenor and bass at the words 'Ave summae aeternitatis' (Ex. 20) and 'Ave Domini filia',[86] and a graceful gymel passage for divided trebles beginning 'Ave plena gratia'.[87] Generally speaking, the part movement is independent, and there is little use made of imitation in any of its forms. Many of the polyphonic lines are quite long and rhapsodic, so that in the five-part sections in particular, the texture is often rather thick and the words somewhat obscured. Nevertheless, it is an impressive work, and worthy of close attention.

Gaude plurimum shares many of the characteristics of *Ave Dei patris filia*, though there are signs of a more mature hand at work. It is not quite as long as its companion, and, although similarly florid in style, the texture is rather more transparent. The text, again Marian, is long and elaborate, and the composer has wisely

---

84 J. H. Parker: *Statutes of the Colleges of Oxford*, Vol. II.
85 Eton College MS. and British Museum: Add. MS. 29246 respectively.
86 T.C.M. Vol. III, pp. 62 and 66 respectively.
87 *Ibid.*, pp. 67-9.

Ex. 20

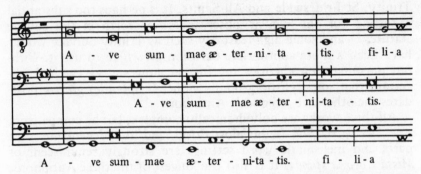

adopted a mainly syllabic treatment of the words, reserving his melismatic writing for the final 'Amen'. Many of the long polyphonic phrases similar to those found in the earlier Antiphon are now subdivided into shorter ones separated by punctuating rests; and imitation, both initial and internal, occurs fairly frequently. Contrast is created by varied vocal scoring and by the antiphonal use of upper and lower voices, as in the section beginning with the words 'Eundem igitur'.[88]

O splendor gloriae is the most mature of the three large-scale Antiphons. It is shorter than the other two, though the text is almost as long and elaborate as that of *Gaude plurimum*. Once again the composer has treated the words syllabically, save for the final 'Amen', where he allows his polyphony to flower in well-contrived melismatic phrases of great beauty. Just as the compositional techniques used in *Gaude plurimum* were in advance of those found in *Ave Dei patris filia*, so the craftsmanship in *O splendor gloriae* is superior to that of *Gaude plurimum*. This is particularly noticeable in the five-part sections, which are musically more transparent and texturally clearer than in the other two Antiphons. The success of the work also results from Taverner's extensive use of imitation, which plays so important a role in this piece that at times it is the controlling factor in the entire musical structure. This can be seen in the final section beginning at the words 'te prece precamur'[89] (Ex. 21).

Of the short Votive Antiphons, only *Mater Christi* has come down to us complete. The sole surviving source of four of the other settings, namely *Ave Maria, Fac nobis, Sancte Deus* and *Sub tuum praesidium*, is a mid-sixteenth century set of part-

88 T.C.M. Vol. III, p. 88.
89 *Ibid.*, p. 108.

Ex.21

books[90] of which the treble and tenor are missing. We are therefore left with only three of the original five voice-parts of these

90 Appendix, paragraph 21.

Antiphons. This is particularly regrettable in the case of *Fac nobis*, whose gracefully shaped phrases show it to have been a very beautiful work. It is also the longest of the four settings and the most florid, with imitation a regular feature of the style. The other three Antiphons are simpler in construction, with short homophonic passages alternating with polyphony, involving a limited use of imitation. The word-setting is mainly syllabic, with an occasional melismatic flowering like that at 'Jesus' in the final section of *Ave Maria*.[91]

Stylistically all four works could date from Taverner's years at Oxford, and records show that two of them might well have been written to satisfy the requirements of Cardinal College. According to the statutes of the college,[92] at seven o'clock each evening the choristers proceeded to the Chapel, and there, together with their choirmaster and some of the chaplains and clerks, sang a polyphonic setting of the Antiphon *Salve Regina*. Then, after prayer, they knelt and sang 'solemniter' the Antiphon *Ave Maria*, which was divided into three sections, and punctuated by the ringing of a bell. This completed, the company then moved into the Chapel nave, and sang in polyphony another Antiphon, *Sancte Deus*, whilst kneeling before the crucifix.[93]

These College requirements certainly provide a very convincing reason for Taverner's short and relatively simple setting of *Sancte Deus*, which would have been both practicable and appropriate for regular evening observances. The same might be said of *Ave Maria*, which was composed in a three-sectional form with two strongly marked internal cadences, the first after the initial salutation and the second before the final word 'Jesus', allowing for the customary bell-ringing. This leaves us with the thought that a *Salve Regina* Antiphon might be amongst the lost Taverner works, for no such setting by him has survived.

Another Antiphon that might have been composed for use at Cardinal College is *Christe Jesu pastor bone*. This work has previously been mentioned in connection with the Mass *Small Devotion*,[94] parts of which are constructed upon phrases borrowed from this Antiphon. It is found in two manuscript sources, namely the Peterhouse part-books[95] containing the four short Antiphons already described, and a later collection copied by John

91 T.C.M. Vol. III, p. 134.
92 J. H. Parker: *Statutes of the Colleges of Oxford*, Vol. II.
93 Harrison: *Music in Mediaeval Britain*, op. cit.
94 See pp. 64-5.
95 Appendix, paragraph 21.

Baldwin, and preserved at Christ Church, Oxford.[96] Unfortunately the tenor book is missing in each case, but the Editors of *Tudor Church Music* have made a very convincing reconstruction of the work.[97]

The text of the earlier source consists of two neat and compact stanzas, the first an antiphon in the Name of Jesus, and the second a prayer for Henry VIII. In an interesting and imaginative explanation of the possible history of *Christe Jesu*,[98] Denis Stevens suggests that the first stanza was originally in memory of St William, a twelfth century Archbishop of York,[99] and might have read:

O *Wilhelme* pastor bone
Cleri *pater* et patrone
Mundum nobis in agone
Confer opem et depone
Vitae sordes et coronae
Coelestis da *gaudia*.

We know from the Statutes of Cardinal College that St William was commemorated daily in one of the three antiphons sung after Vespers and Compline, and it is quite feasible that its text could have taken the above form. Stevens also goes on to suggest that the prayer of the second stanza was not originally for the King, but for another Archbishop of York, namely Thomas Wolsey (1514-30), and possibly began:

Fundatorem specialem
Serva *Thomam Cardinalem*. . .

After the fall of Wolsey and the re-founding in 1532 of his Oxford College under Henry VIII, the text of the Antiphon was amended, with the Monarch's name replacing that of the deposed Cardinal, and Jesus Christ that of St William, whose memory would have little if any significance for the King.[100] These changes were made by a simple substitution for each of the italicized words in the above quotations, thus stanza 1:

O *Christe Jesu* pastor bone
Cleri *fautor* et patrone
Semper nobis in agone
Confer opem et depone
Vitae sordes et coronae
Coelestis da *gloriam*.

96 *Ibid.*, paragraph 18.
97 T.C.M. Vol. III, pp. 73ff.
98 *Die Musik in Geschichte und Gegenwart*, Vol. XIII.
99 Died in 1154; canonised in 1226.
100 N.B. Henry's name is replaced by that of Elizabeth in the later manuscript source of the Antiphon (ref. Appendix, paragraph 18).

Stanza 2:

> Fundatorem specialem
> Serva *regem nunc Henricum*. . .

Whether or not we accept this very logical argument, the work would seem to date from the Oxford years. It is the entire opposite of the large-scale festal antiphon, and possesses a quiet dignity all its own. It is mainly homophonic in style, and the words are treated syllabically throughout except for the cadential phrase. The antiphonal use of upper and lower voices occurs at the beginning of each stanza of the text, and occasional use is made of imitation. The individual voice parts move in predominantly smooth, arch-shaped phrases, each within a small range of notes. At times the texture has an austerity reminiscent of the *Playn Song Mass*, as in the opening of the second stanza, 'Fundatorem specialem'.[101]

The only short Votive Antiphon that has survived intact is *Mater Christi*, which was mentioned earlier as providing material for the construction of the Parody Mass of the same name. It is found in numerous manuscripts from the mid-sixteenth century onwards, and appears in one or two places adapted to English words.[102] According to a companion note to Philip Brett's edition of the work, it is not a Marian setting as might be assumed from the initial lines of the text, for this opening 'is followed by what appears to be a prayer for grace through the receiving of the Blessed Sacrament'. For this reason the Antiphon might have been used during the celebration of the Mass.

The work falls into quite clearly defined sections coinciding with the verse-form of the text, and the words are set in a mainly syllabic style with a final melismatic 'Amen'. It is more polyphonic than *Christe Jesu*, but there are several homophonic passages, and antiphony plays an important part in its construction. Imitation is a regular feature of the writing, and at times comes close to canon. Such a passage occurs at the words 'Quin et nostras'[103] which shows clearly the influence of the Netherlands School, as does the section beginning 'salutari'[104] with its well managed five-part imitative entries (Ex. 22).

The two short Marian settings, *Prudens virgo* and *Virgo pura*, both for three-part lower voices, are found in an early seventeenth

---

101 T.C.M. Vol. III, p. 75.
102 Appendix, paragraphs 14 and 20.
103 T.C.M. Vol. III, p. 97.
104 *Ibid.*, p. 95.

Ex.22

century commonplace book[105] of John Baldwin. Although each Antiphon is complete in itself, it seems likely that they are both opening sections of more substantial works since the material in each case has the potential for more extended growth. This is especially true of *Prudens virgo*, which is written in an attractive melismatic style and has an almost festal ring about it.

105   Appendix, paragraph 11.

Miscellaneous Works

INCLUDING CANTICLES, RESPONDS AND VERSES

In his five-part *Te Deum*, Taverner has set only the even-numbered verses in polyphony, so that the work would be performed *alternatim*, with the odd-numbered verses sung to plainchant. The only manuscript source of the piece is a set of part-books copied by John Baldwin and dated 1581,[106] of which the tenor is missing. The loss of this book is not serious, however, for it has been a relatively straightforward task to reconstruct the tenor line by simply inserting the plainsong melody as a monorhythmic cantus firmus. The only problem arises in the verse 'Aeterna fac'[107] when the chant goes into the bass.

The writing is florid in style and the mood festal in spirit, but there is a controlled expression of praise that points to the work being a product of Taverner's mature years. In view of the *alternatim* structure, it falls naturally into self-contained sections, several of which begin imitatively and end with a melisma on the final word. Although the imitation is often close and the scoring is for full choir throughout, the part-writing is always clear and the text never obscured. Ex. 23 is a typical passage from the *Te Deum*, showing imitation, smooth and spontaneously constructed contrapuntal lines, and a masterly treatment of discord in the second bar.

The three *Magnificat* settings are also *alternatim* works, but this time the odd-numbered verses have been treated polyphonically whilst the even ones would be sung to plainchant by the cantors. Only the four-part setting for men's voices alone has survived in its complete form,[108] whilst the five-part setting, whose sole manuscript source is the Peterhouse part-books,[109] lacks a tenor part, and the one in six parts has lost most of its treble.[110] All three settings give the impression of having been composed prior to the *Te Deum*. The six-part one in particular has a textural layout and an exuberance closely akin to *Missa Corona spinea*.

---

106 Appendix, paragraph 18.
107 T.C.M. Vol. III, p. 31.
108 Appendix, paragraph 4.
109 *Ibid.*, paragraph 21.
110 A little of the treble part has been rescued from a Christ Church, Oxford manuscript which contains an excerpt from the 6-part *Magnificat* (Appendix, paragraph 17).

Ex.23

The four- and six-part settings are each built upon a cantus firmus taken from the psalm-tones, a group of eight Gregorian melodies corresponding to the eight ecclesiastical modes, and used for psalm-singing during the Office. In both cases the chants are given to the tenor voice in long-note values which are often embellished at the cadence. The four-part *Magnificat* is based fairly strictly upon Tone VI, whilst the six-part one has as its cantus firmus Tone I which is treated with considerable freedom. The five-part setting, with its missing tenor voice, presents problems since none of the psalm-tones appears to fill the gap convincingly.

Texturally all three works demonstrate the same elements of contrast already met in the Festal Masses, namely adjacent passages for full and reduced choir, occasional mensural change, and antiphony. There are several examples of long melismatic phrases on single syllables, especially in the six-part setting, but beyond the opening and closing sections of the piece there is little full-choir polyphony, so that the words are rarely lost amidst the florid part-writing. Imitation is found in each *Magnificat*, and, although it is unwise to base the chronology of a work upon the presence of a single technical device, the extent to which it is used in the five-part setting points to it possibly being the latest of the three works.

Taverner's music for the Office Responds constitutes an important part of his entire output, and shows him engaged in the art of combining free composition with the set forms of the liturgy. This is successfully accomplished in the works that are built upon the monorhythmic cantus firmus principle, and written for alternating plainsong and polyphony. These include *Audivi vocem de caelo*, *In pace in idipsum*, and the three settings of *Dum transisset Sabbatum*. In the first two pieces, Taverner has followed fifteenth-century practice by treating polyphonically those parts of the text that are usually' sung by soloists, namely the opening phrase, the verse, and, in the second respond, the *Gloria Patri*, leaving the choral sections in plainsong. Thus, in performance, *Audivi vocem* would begin with the initial word sung in polyphony, after which the choir would continue[111] the opening sentences, 'vocem. . .sapientissimae. Oleum. . .advenerit', to plainchant. Polyphony would then return with the verse, 'Media nocte. . .sponsus venit', and the choir would complete the work with the last part of their earlier passage, 'Oleum. . .advenerit', to plainsong.

Audivi vocem is the Eighth Respond at Matins on the Feast of All Saints,[112] and Taverner's setting is in florid polyphony built upon the plainsong. It is scored for four-part upper voices, two trebles and two meanes, the significance of which lies in the practice on All Saints' Day of boys being the principal participants at this point in the Office.[113] After one boy had read the eighth lesson, the five virgins referred to therein would be represented by a group of five choirboys who would then sing the Respond,

---

111 From the double bar in T.C.M. Vol. III, p. 35.
112 Antiphonale Sarisburiense, Pl. 567.
113 *The Use of Sarum*, Ed. Harrison, pp. 120-21.

the first part while facing the altar and the second part (from 'Ecce sponsus') before the choir.

On the question of scoring, the 'Gyffard' part-books,[114] sole manuscript source of the work, state that the first meane is an optional part[115] added by William Whytbroke (c.1495-c.1568), who was a chaplain at Cardinal College at the time of Taverner's appointment. Close examination of the piece shows that this could be correct, for whilst the style of the added part does not conflict with that of the other three florid lines, it does occasionally get in the way of the second meane. Furthermore, its unusual pairing at the distance of a third with other voices at imitative places like 'Media' and 'sponsus'[116] points to the work of another hand. In short, the work as a whole is perfectly satisfactory without the first meane, even though the texture is somewhat thin at times, which may be the reason for Whytbroke's efforts to fill out the harmony.

There is one puzzling instance of divided second trebles at the word 'Ecce' which indicates a deviation from the general rule of using solo voices for the polyphonic sections of a respond, and raises the question of how many boys were actually used to sing this work. Without wishing to add to the existing confusion surrounding Taverner research, the present writer would tentatively suggest that the answer to this question might lie in the distribution of the cantus firmus, which in the opening and closing sections of the piece is in the first treble, and in the middle section in the second. Whenever it appears, it is in long phrases of sustained semibreves, which poses breathing problems for the solo voice if the phrases are to remain unbroken. With two boys to each treble part, however, one of them might have been detailed to sing the freely composed lines, which are always in short, concise phrases, with the second boy assisting in unison whenever the cantus firmus occurs, thus strengthening and maintaining the linear character of the chant. These two pairs of voices plus one boy singing the second meane (which never has the plainsong melody) would then be adequate for the performance of the original three-part setting, and might even constitute the five choirboys detailed in the rubrics for All Saints' Day to represent 'quinque virgines'.

The sole Respond sung at Compline was *In pace in idipsum*, and that only between the first Sunday in Lent and Passion Sunday.[117]

114 Appendix, paragraph 4.
115 i.e. 'pars ad placitum'.
116 T.C.M. Vol. III, pp. 35 and 36 respectively.
117 Harrison: *The Use of Sarum*, pp. 62 and 98.

Taverner's setting of this text is found in the same manuscript source as *Audivi vocem*, namely the 'Gyffard' part-books,[118] where it is scored for 'iij men and a child'. It is built upon similar lines to its companion Respond but with the cantus firmus always in the treble, supported by three florid parts beneath. In performance the opening polyphonic phrase, 'In pace',[119] would be sung by solo voices followed by the choir singing 'in idipsum dormiam et requiescam' to plainsong. Polyphony would then be resumed in the verse 'Si dedero somnum. . .dormitationem', to which the choir would reply, again to plainsong, 'Dormiam et requiescam'. After this the soloists would sing the four-part 'Gloria Patri', and the piece would conclude with the complete text, 'In pace. . .et requiescam', chanted by the choir.

The musical style of the work is similar to that of *Audivi vocem*, though the individual voice-parts follow rather more graceful contours. The texture is lucid, and the various compositional devices, including imitation of the cantus firmus at the beginning, and sequence in the cadence bars, are well managed.

Dum transisset Sabbatum is the Respond to the third lesson at Matins on Easter Sunday. It was also used daily during Easter Week and on subsequent Sundays until Ascension.[120] Taverner's three settings of the text comprise a five-part one,[121] a four-part version of the same,[122] and another five-part one numbered II in the Tudor Church Music Series.[123] Both five-part Responds are found in the Christ Church, Oxford collection compiled by John Baldwin and dated 1581[124], but the only complete source of the first one is another Christ Church manuscript of the same period, copied in the main by a certain Robert Dow.[125] The other five-part work also has a second source in a book of vocal and instrumental music dating from about 1578,[126] but the four-part version has survived in only one manuscript, namely the 'Gyffard' part-books.[127]

In all three settings, Taverner reverses the structural scheme used in *Audivi vocem* and *In pace* by writing polyphonically for the choir and leaving the solo sections in plainchant. The same process

118 Appendix, paragraph 4.
119 T.C.M. Vol. III, p. 48, (first five bars).
120 *The Use of Sarum*, II, p. 71.
121 T.C.M. Vol. III, p. 37.
122 *Ibid.*, p. 40.
123 *Ibid.*, p. 43.
124 Appendix, paragraph 18.
125 *Ibid.*, paragraph 19.
126 *Ibid.*, paragraph 8.
127 *Ibid.*, paragraph 4.

has already been noted in the two *Alleluias*,[128] and it had previously been used by composers for over half a century in music for the Lady Mass. Taverner, however, appears to have been the first to introduce it into a respond. In performance, therefore, each setting of *Dum transisset* would begin with the *incipit* sung by the soloists to plainchant, followed by 'Sabbatum. . .aromata, ut venientes ungerent Jesum. Alleluia, alleluia,' sung polyphonically by the choir. The verse 'Et valide. . .iam sole' would then be chanted, after which the choir would sing the latter part of the Respond (from 'ut venientes'). Next would come the 'Gloria Patri', sung to plainsong, and the work would end with choral 'Alleluias'.

Stylistically the three works appear to belong to Taverner's Oxford years, though the second of the five-part settings contains the most mature writing, and points to a date fractionally later than the other two. In each case the cantus firmus is in the tenor voice, around which the remaining parts weave smooth, well-shaped phrases of great beauty. The composer strikes a happy balance between a syllabic and melismatic treatment of the words, and there is a remarkable textual clarity, even in the long stretches of five-part polyphony. Effective use of imitation is found in the first setting at the word 'aromata'[129] (Ex. 24).

Hodie nobis caelorum rex is the First Respond at Matins on Christmas Day, from which Taverner set only the verse *Gloria in excelsis Deo*,[130] scoring it for four-part boys' voices, two trebles and two meanes. The special significance of this scoring lies in the fact that, during this Office, the boys are directed to represent the angels referred to in the Respond by standing in some elevated position near the altar holding lighted candles.[131] The composer takes this observance of the rubrics one step further by adopting an almost festal style of writing in which long melismatic phrases, appropriate to the sentiment of the words, accompany the cantus firmus disposed monorhythmically in the second treble. There is occasional use of imitation, but the free exuberant style and the almost continuous four-part texture are indicative of an early stage in Taverner's career.

Technically speaking, *Sospitati dedit aegros* is a prose — that is, an interpolation, which in this case is into the Respond *Ex eius*

128   p. 73f.
129   T.C.M. Vol. III, p. 38.
130   Sole MS. source Appendix, paragraph 4.
131   *The Use of Sarum*, II, p. 30.

Ex. 24

tumba[132] sung on the Feast of St Nicholas (6 December)[133] A prose was generally confined in its use to First Vespers on certain Saints' Days, and performed *alternatim* between a small group of

132 Between the words 'Et debilis quisque' and 'regreditur'.
133 *Breviarum Sarum*, III, p. 36.

singers and the full choir. In the case of *Sospitati*, however, the text was inserted into the Ninth Respond at Matins, and Taverner's setting is in choral polyphony throughout. It occurs in several manuscripts from the late sixteenth and early seventeenth centuries, of which all but one were originally part of the Edward Paston library.[134] It has been suggested that the work was written to mark the Feast Day of the Fraternity of St Nicholas, the London Gild whose membership list in 1514 included a John Taverner. Obviously this hinges on whether or not the Bede Roll entry refers to the composer; but the music of *Sospitati dedit aegros* is written in a relatively early style, and is therefore consistent with this theory.

Structurally the work resembles a 'variation-chain'[135], since Taverner produces a different setting for each of the eight verses, after which he has added the final phrase of the Respond, 'sospes regreditur'. Some verses are written in five-part polyphony for full choir, and others in three or four parts, producing varied sonorities similar to those noted in his settings of the Mass. Plainsong plays a unifying role in the construction of the work, sometimes used as a cantus firmus, as in verse 6 and in the 'sospes regreditur' passage,[136] and at other times as a foundation for imitation and canonic treatment as in verses 2 and 4 respectively.[137] In contrast, verses 7 and 8 are freely composed without reference to the chant.

Ecce Mater is the verse of the Processional Respond *Ecce carissimi* which was sung before High Mass on the three Sundays leading up to Lent. Its sole source is the John Baldwin manuscript of 1581,[138] and it is the only surviving two-part sacred work by Taverner. The scoring for a countertenor and a bass voice shows the composer's strict observance of the rubrics which state that the verse should be sung by two clerks.[139] The work is not built upon plainsong, and consists of two freely composed florid lines employing simple points of imitation and so disposed as to produce a remarkable fullness of sound.

Three other verse settings by Taverner, all of which appear to be excerpts from complete *alternatim* settings,[140] have come down to us in an early seventeenth-century commonplace book copied

134 See p. 39.
135 *New Oxford History of Music*, Vol. III, pp. 343-4.
136 T.C.M. Vol. III, p. 113.
137 *Ibid.*, pp. 110 and 111.
138 Appendix, paragraph 18.
139 *Processionale ad Usum Sarum*, Gregg Reprint 1969, p. 24, and *The Use of Sarum*, II, p. 157.
140 Harrison: *Music in Medieval Britain*, p. 392.

by John Baldwin.[141] The first one, *Jesu spes poenitentibus*, is the third verse of the Sequence *Dulcis Jesu memoria* for the Mass of the Holy Name of Jesus.[142] It is scored for treble, counter-tenor and tenor, and consists of two outer parts moving in a simple and rather undistinguished manner alongside a mono-rhythmic cantus firmus in the middle voice, which is treated decoratively at the cadence.

The second setting, *Traditur militibus*, is the sixth verse of the Sequence *Coenam cum discipulis* for the Mass of the Five Wounds of Jesus.[143] The work is also in three parts, but this time for meane, tenor and bass. Again the cantus firmus is in the middle voice but in semibreves instead of the usual breves. Once more the outer parts trace simple, steadily moving curves around the monorhythmic chant, with slightly increased activity in the cadential phrase.

Finally, *Tam peccatum* is the fourth verse of the Tract *Dulce nomen Jesu Christe* for the Jesus Mass sung during Lent.[144] It is scored for treble, tenor and bass, and is built upon a short musical phrase which is stated first in breves, then in semibreves, and thirdly in minims, placed in each case in the highest voice. Meanwhile the lower parts sing freely composed lines employing simple points of imitation. This verse setting is undoubtedly superior to the other two, and even within its short span the music has a noticeable momentum, and there is a strong drive to the cadence.

One more apparently sacred work remains to be examined, namely *Quemadmodum* which has been, and still is, a problem since it lacks any text in all its three manuscript sources.[145] Even the sources themselves which include a set of part-books copied by John Baldwin, are unhelpful and give no indication of the purpose for which the piece was composed. Writing over fifty years ago,[146] H. B. Collins maintained that the work was a setting of the first two verses of Psalm 41(42), which in the Vulgate begins 'Quemadmodum desiderat cervus', and even went so far as

141 Appendix, paragraph 11.
142 Harrison: *Music in Medieval Britain*, p. 392, and *Missale Sarum*, column 850.
143 Harrison: *Music in Medieval Britain*, p. 393, and *Missale Sarum*, column 752.
144 *Ibid.*, column 848.
145 Appendix, paragraphs 8, 18 and 32.
146 In *Music and Letters* VI (1925), p. 316.

to show how the text could be fitted to the music. Although the title is the only evidence in support of this view, no more convincing explanation has since been offered and at this stage one can only accept Collins's theory, though still with an open mind.

Whatever the purpose, the work itself is a masterful piece of writing, and is certainly a product of Taverner's mature years. It is scored for six 'voices',[147] and falls into two self-contained parts of approximately the same length. The work is built upon short, rhythmically varied phrases, most of them treated imitatively (Ex. 25).[148] The continuous six-part writing is liberally punctuated by short rests between phrases so that the texture remains remarkably transparent throughout. An interesting and effective link is created between the two halves of the work by starting the second one (Ex. 27, p. 103) with an inversion of the ascending four-note phrase used at the beginning of the piece. In addition to this, there is a kinship between several of the phrases through the motif of a rising or falling fourth, either with or without intervening notes. In short, it is regrettable if so accomplished a

Ex.25

147 The term is used in the sense of 'parts', and a theory that cannot be totally rejected is that *Quemadmodum* is an instrumental composition (see Appendix, paragraph 18).

148 T.C.M. Vol. III, p. 117, bars 22ff.

Ex. 25 cont.

work as this should suffer neglect, and whilst in the absence of a text it may not prove 'apt for voyces', it could successfully be kept alive by viols.

The Secular Songs

In addition to the wealth of sacred music by Taverner, four secular songs have also come down to us. They are found in a collection of *XX Songes*, whose sole manuscript source originally comprised four small part-books printed in London in 1530. Of these the bass part[149] alone has survived along with three fragments of the treble and meane,[150] so that unfortunately only one of the Taverner works has been preserved intact.[151] All four of his songs are settings of love lyrics, a popular form in early Tudor Court circles, and although they could date from as late as his Oxford years, it is more likely that they were produced during the previous decade. This view is supported by the fact that they are in company with songs by composers who were connected with the Henrician Court prior to 1520.[152] Their inclusion in the book of *XX Songes* adds further weight to the theory that Taverner spent some time in London during his early career.

The one complete song is a setting for two voices of a punctuation-poem *In women is rest peas and pacience*. This type of poem is a play upon words which produce a double meaning dependent upon the position of the punctuation-marks. Taverner appears to have enjoyed himself in his playful treatment of the text, which is set in the Ionian Mode in a florid, free contrapuntal style. There are long melismas for the two voices moving in parallel thirds and sixths, and the occasional use of simple imitation.

Little can be said about the other songs except that, in their incomplete state, they still give the impression of having been constructed on sound lines. The most elaborate setting is *The bella, the bella*, a carol of four verses, each with a refrain, and scored for three or four voices in a lively, sportive style. *Love wyll I and leve* is a direct descendant of the mediaeval courtly song. It was a three-part setting, and, from an examination of the surviving bass line, it appears to have been treated in a somewhat plaintive manner, with a final section in more animated triplet

149 Appendix, paragraph 33a.
150 *Ibid.*, paragraph 33b.
151 In a study of these songs, D. S. Josephson has made a reconstruction of *The bella, the bella* using the MSS. quoted in the Appendix, paragraph 33 together with some fragments forming end pages to a seventeenth-century MS. at present housed in New York Public Library, ref. Drexel MSS. 4180-85.
152 Including Thomas Ashwell, William Cornyshe, Robert Cowper, Robert Fayrfax, Robert Jones and Richard Pygot.

rhythm, a characteristic of Tudor writing. Less spirited, too, is *Mi hart my mynde*, a three-part 'mistress song' composed in a mostly syllabic style in the transposed Dorian Mode. Again, judging from the bass line alone, it appears to have been a work of grace and beauty, and one in which interval repetition, ostinato and sequence all play a unifying role

In the final assessment, the four secular songs may very well carry the hallmarks of juvenilia, but they possess a certain youthful freshness and an endearing charm, as well as revealing yet another facet of Taverner's creative mind.

PART III
TAVERNER'S MUSICAL STYLE

John Taverner's life and work falls into the framework of a musical England that was still firmly grounded in the Gothic tradition. Although the Renaissance is often quoted as having its beginnings in the mid-fifteenth century, it is impossible to draw a date-line that will apply equally to all countries of Western civilization, or even to different composers working simultaneously within the same domain. Certainly elements of Renaissance thinking began to appear regularly in the music of English and Continental composers a generation or more before Taverner's time, but rather than replacing earlier practices, they were generally grafted onto a stem that was still rooted in the Gothic style. In the early Flemish School, for example, Obrecht (c.1453-1505) helped to prepare the soil for the growth of sixteenth-century techniques through his feeling for tonality and harmonic progression, and in this country Fayrfax (1464-1521) anticipated future change in his leanings towards a less florid polyphony than that of his predecessors; but in each case these new trends are found within a mode of expression that is still essentially mediaeval.

The features that separate Renaissance style from that of the Middle Ages stem largely from a basic textural difference. In the earlier period, part writing was governed by contrast, a quality partly resulting from the method of composition, which consisted of adding to an initial melody other voice parts, one at a time, with little apparent regard for the total polyphonic effect or the overall harmonic progression. In the predominantly three-part texture of the day there was at times considerable discordancy between the parts that was often heightened by the juxtaposing of sacred and secular melodies and the simultaneous use of different texts, sometimes in different languages.

In the Renaissance, however, the aim was to blend, and although contrast was by no means absent, it was cultivated on a different

97

plane and within an overall euphonious texture. A polyphonic composition was conceived as a whole, and not as a succession of parts added one at a time; the individual voices were more closely related to each other, both in character and tone colour, than previously. The contrapuntal lines were all of equal importance, though there was an increasing dependence upon the bass as a foundation for the harmony, which was triadic, and consisted mainly of root position and first inversion chords. Tension was created by a systematic use of dissonance often derived from suspensions. Compositional techniques like imitation, canon, sequence, ostinato, homophony and antiphony all played a major role in Renaissance style; in fact the first of these was the very life-blood of sixteenth-century polyphony. Textual clarity was cultivated in vocal works, and there was a tendency to make music reflect the meaning of the words. Finally there was an awareness of the need for structural balance within a piece, which is particularly noticeable in extended settings such as the Mass and large-scale antiphons. It should be emphasised that these features are not entirely peculiar to Renaissance style — in fact many of them are found in mediaeval pieces — but whereas in the latter they occur rather sporadically, during the sixteenth century they became standard practice.

The actual transition from Gothic to Renaissance composition was a very gradual process, involving an extended period of overlap which in England amounted to close on a hundred years. The reason for this is that mediaeval principles had become so firmly established through centuries of practice that it required some considerable time and effort before the old *modus operandi* gave way to the full flowering of Renaissance ideas. The transition began with the new techniques first being grafted on to the basic Gothic style and then being assimilated into it. As time went on, these new elements began to assume a more active role, until they finally ousted the old mediaeval practices and became themselves the natural and spontaneous mode of expression. The ultimate advent of the Renaissance was therefore determined not so much by date as by musical style, and in England the last traces of the Gothic tradition disappeared only with the introduction of the reformed liturgy in the mid-sixteenth century.

All this may account for the fact that Taverner has been described as a composer working in an archaic style, but that is not an accurate assessment. It is true that he was nurtured in a musical climate that had a strong and lasting effect upon his writing, but much of his later work shows a readiness to try out new compositional skills, and to absorb them into his language. There is in fact an almost Janus-like quality about his mature works which, through his environment, look back to the generation of Fayrfax and Cornyshe, and, through his own inclinations, anticipate the High Renaissance. It is therefore no easy matter to summarise Taverner's style, or to fit into historical sequence the work of a composer whose output was more varied than that of any of his contemporaries, English or Continental. Perhaps the only general observation that can be made at this stage is that his later works show a distinct tendency towards simplicity and a more direct form of expression, in marked contrast to the florid and complex character of his earlier writing. His stylistic development, however, can best be traced by considering separately the various ingredients of the art of composition: melody, harmony, polyphonic techniques and form.

The musical texture of Taverner's early work is characterized by the strongly independent nature of the part-writing, with the accent upon contrast rather than blend. The different voices pursue their individual courses in elaborately-shaped florid phrases which usually have little or no melodic relationship with each other. They are also rhythmically independent, with musical and textual stress occurring at irregular intervals in each voice, creating at times a complicated polyphonic web of sound. At first, imitation is introduced incidentally rather than as a structural device or as a means of unifying a passage, and rarely extends beyond the initial few notes of a phrase. There are no systematic attempts to make the music fit the mood of the text, and words are often obscured, and even distorted, by the complex melismatic part-movement. In short, these features add up to a style that is common to most Tudor composers, and that has its roots in the traditions established through the work of previous generations.

As time goes on, however, we find Taverner cultivating a simpler and more transparent texture in marked contrast with the continued complexity of some of his contemporaries. He still maintains Gothic principles in the individuality of his part writing, but there is an increased and conscious use of such techniques as imitation, canonic treatment, sequence and repetition, all of which play their part in co-ordinating the separate polyphonic strands of a work into one homogeneous whole. Obviously there are greater opportunities for developing a simpler and more direct mode of expression in the shorter and non-festal settings, but even in *Missa Gloria tibi Trinitas* and the jubilant Antiphon *O splendor gloriae*

99

there is a tendency to create a texture in which the individual voices are less at variance with each other than previously, and are given a certain degree of interdependence through the use of imitation and phrase-repetition. In these and similar works, the polyphony is still florid in style, especially in those sections scored for reduced choir or for solo voices. However, the adoption of a less complicated rhythmic scheme and the punctuation of long, flowing contrapuntal lines by well-placed rests with occasional 'internal' imitation all contribute towards increased musical and textual clarity. A recurring feature in Taverner's festal writing is his fondness for the progressive shortening of note values, resulting in an acceleration at the approach to a main cadence. This treatment is not peculiar to his style of writing, but it is never used by other early Tudor composers with quite the same assurance or with such telling effect.

Taverner's most direct and concise utterances are found in the *Meane Mass* and in that study in musical economy, the *Playn Song Mass*, and one is tempted for different reasons to place both these works late in the composer's career. The former has all the signs of the mature artist, and furthermore anticipates those qualities that we have come to associate with the golden age of polyphony. Although still mainly florid in style, the texture is transparent throughout, and imitation has now become the prime factor in controlling the musical growth of a passage. The *Playn Song Mass* in its austerity also shows a new and almost experimental mode of expression at a time when other composers were still writing in a mainly florid idiom, though it might also have its origins in its author's leaning towards a simpler form of worship.

The freedom and exuberance of Taverner's melodic style shows it to be a direct descendant of mediaeval compositional practice, and only in such works as the *Meane Mass* and *Quemadmodum* does he approach the grace and fluency of the late sixteenth-century masters. His melodies are constructed from mainly arch-shaped phrases in a predominantly conjunct movement which, in some of his festal settings, develops into long, animated scalic runs which cut through the neighbouring voice parts. Melodic leaps do not generally exceed a perfect fifth except in the bass where octave shifts occur from time to time.

Sequence plays an important part in melodic construction, particularly in highly melismatic passages where it can help to shape a long, rhapsodic phrase, and also provide a powerful musical drive. It is puzzling why so simple yet so effective a device should not have found a regular place in the sacred works either of Taverner's predecessors or of his contemporaries, for he himself introduced it as early as the *Western Wind* Mass and made it a recurrent feature of his festal settings. It often occurs in the bass part of a 'tutti' passage where it helps to provide a secure foundation for the upper voices. A good example of this can be found at the first 'miserere nobis' in the *Agnus Dei* from *Missa Gloria tibi Trinitas*,[1] where the bass line of the entire section is built upon short phrases, each of them treated sequentially (Ex. 26). Considerable freedom can accompany the use of sequence: for instance, the interval of rise or fall may vary at each repetition of the motif or phrase (as in the third and sixth bars of Ex. 26), and the repetitions themselves may be separated by rests. An example of double sequence can be seen in the two-part melismatic treatment of the last syllable of 'sepultus' in the *Credo* of *O Michael*,[2] where the lower voice sings six statements of a four-note motif, a step higher at each repetition, against the upper voice's two statements of a longer phrase.

Sequence is not the only form of phrase-repetition used by Taverner; several examples of both ostinato and antiphony have already been quoted. The former is not an important feature of his technique, however, nor is it found in its strict form in the more mature works. By its very nature, with repeated statements at the same pitch and in the same voice, it appears to impose too many restrictions upon the accompanying polyphonic parts, and whilst it might serve as a unifying device, it can also act as a brake upon the musical drive.

Ex. 26

1 T.C.M. Vol. I, pp. 151-2.
2 *Ibid.*, p. 208.

Antiphonal repetition seems to be more acceptable, and this occurs in a number of Taverner's shorter settings including *Missa Mater Christi*, the *Meane Mass* and *Small Devotion*. It is most frequently encountered in five-part textures where a phrase sung by the treble and meane is repeated by the lower three voices, the countertenor taking the original upper part an octave lower, and the tenor or bass the other part, with a free counterpoint added for the third voice. Another way of handling antiphony in five-part writing is by contrasting the three upper voices with the three lower ones, the middle line acting as a treble to one 'choir' and a bass to the other. This treatment can be seen between the phrases 'Domine Deus' and 'Agnus Dei' in the *Gloria* of the *Mater Christi* Mass.[3]

The most sublime and sophisticated form of repetition is of course imitation, a device that took some time to establish itself in this country despite the fact that it had been in regular use by Continental composers long before the Tudor era. Some of Taverner's predecessors, including Fayrfax, had introduced it from time to time, but it never had an important place in their work, nor was it used in any structural capacity. In view of its relatively late appearance in English composition, the extent and manner of its use have become valuable means of determining the chronology of early sixteenth-century music in this country: although it is not the only factor that must be examined (other elements include texture, word setting and harmonic progression) it has proved to be a useful guide in dating many Tudor works.

There are several different forms of imitation, both strict and free, and numerous ways in which it can be deployed in polyphonic composition. Taverner's imitation can be of the initial or internal variety — that is, it can occur at the beginning of a phrase or during the course of one. The former is the more common, and can vary from its occasional appearance in such works as *Missa O Michael* and *Ave Dei patris filia* to more regular usage in *Gloria tibi Trinitas, Gaude plurimum* and other products of the Oxford years, until it ultimately becomes a prime factor in the shaping of complete contrapuntal passages in such mature writing as the *Meane Mass* and *O splendor gloriae*. Generally speaking, imitative entries in the early- and middle-period works are at the unison, the octave or the fifth, but as time goes on they can be found at any interval. They can also be very close in some of the later pieces, as in the second half of *Quemadmodum* where some of the entries are only a beat apart (Ex. 27).

3 *Ibid.*, p. 101.

Ex.27

The initial form of imitation is more often associated with syllabic word setting, whilst the internal variety is generally found within a melismatic style of writing. The latter begins to appear with regularity in *Gloria tibi Trinitas* (Ex. 6, p. 50), where it provides a sense of direction in the long, rhapsodic phrases with which the music abounds. It also allows the words to be heard more clearly. Its most advanced and controlled use is found in the *Meane Mass*, where the imitative entries are preceded by short, punctuating rests that separate the beginning of one phrase from the end of the previous one and allow the texture to 'breathe'.

There are two other forms of imitation that Taverner helped to pioneer. The first occurs at the beginning of a phrase and involves pairs of voices which enter either simultaneously or successively, and are imitated by another pair entering in the same way an octave above or below. This particular technique had been a feature of the Flemish School during the second half of the fifteenth century, its chief exponent being Josquin des Près (c.1450-1521). In this country, examples of paired entries can occasionally be found in Taverner's Oxford works,[4] but the *Meane Mass* appears to be the first English composition in which the device was used with any degree of regularity (Ex. 15, p. 68).

The second form is more subtle and is found in some of the works built upon plainsong. It involves the imitative use of points derived from the cantus firmus which are either combined polyphonically with the parent phrase or made to anticipate its entry. An example has already been quoted (Ex. 5, p. 49) from the opening movement of *Missa Gloria tibi Trinitas*[5] where each voice, beginning with the bass, imitatively treats the cantus firmus

4 For example in the *Credo* of *Gloria tibi Trinitas*, T.C.M. Vol. I, p. 144, bars 9 and 10.
5 T.C.M. Vol. I, p. 128, bar 1f.

phrase 'Rex coelestis' in the meane part, first anticipating its entry, and then combining with it in six-part counterpoint. In this way the plainsong functions as an integral part of the whole texture, rather than as external scaffolding having no relationship with the remaining parts. Other examples of the imitative use of the cantus firmus can be found in Taverner's later works, notably the second *Dum transisset* and the *Te Deum.*

This brief summary shows that imitation can take on a variety of forms, and that even in the work of a single composer the same technique can be treated in several different ways. But whatever form it takes, the effect of imitation is basically the same, namely the welding together of individual voice-parts by the use of common material. In short, it is one of the most important means by which the independent part-movement of the Gothic tradition was steered into the principal aims of Renaissance musical architecture. Taverner never quite achieved the consummate ease of the late sixteenth-century composers, for in none of his extant works do we find him completely relinquishing the style in which he had been trained. Nevertheless, he was instrumental in carrying the art of imitation forward from its incidental and sporadic use in the music of his immediate predecessors to the beginning of that era when it began to assume a major role as a structural device.

It is significant that canon — that is, continuous imitation — does not generally play an important part in Taverner's writing. Examples of its use have been quoted, particularly in connection with *Missa O Michael*[6] where it appears to have been introduced to demonstrate contrapuntal ingenuity rather than as a structural aid. The English gymel, however, seems to have exerted a stronger influence in view of the number of phrases one finds for divided trebles, especially in the Festal Masses,[7] and although it does not function *per se* as a compositional technique, its value lies in the contrast it creates with the more fully scored neighbouring passages.

The harmonic style of Taverner's early work is little different from that of his immediate predecessors. Triadically based, it is mainly consonant, but with passing dissonances which usually arise from polyphonic decoration and the combination of florid part-movement. In writing for three or more voices, he shows the English composers' predilection for the fullness of sound that

6 p. 54f.
7 For example in *Corona spinea* and *Gloria tibi Trinitas*; references on pp. 43 and 45, and 50 respectively.

results from the use of all three notes of the triad on every main beat. His cadence chords, too, are generally complete, and, unlike his Continental counterparts, he rarely omits the third. His triads are almost always in root position or first inversion, with a marked preference for the former in 'tutti' passages of a majestic or dignified nature. Part-movement avoids the use of parallel perfect fifths and octaves, though reference has repeatedly been made to the frequency with which they occur in the Mass *O Michael* where one can only attribute their presence to inexperience in coping with the rigours of six-part polyphony. The fact that they are so common in that work adds weight to the argument that it was the earliest of the three Festal Masses.

Chordal relationships in Taverner's early writing tended to be somewhat accidental since they were largely determined by the individual part movement, but the links between chords with roots a perfect fourth or fifth apart were obviously recognised. This relationship asserted itself most forcibly in the predominant forms of cadence that we find in his works, namely perfect and plagal. A third form of cadence used by him, and inherited from mediaeval tradition, consisted of an expansion from the first inversion of the leading note triad to the root position of the tonic chord. Occasionally this type of cadence is treated Landini-fashion[8], with the leading note falling a step to the sixth before proceeding to the tonic (Ex. 28), a practice that in this country appears to have ended with Taverner.

Ex.28

As time went on, certain changes became apparent in the harmonic style of both English and Continental composers which marked the beginning of what was ultimately to become the modern major-minor order. The scalic system of the early sixteenth century was still that of the ecclesiastical modes, a system that had initially governed melody alone, and that was perfectly acceptable in mediaeval compositional practice. When applied to Renaissance harmony, however, it was less successful as it often created angularity in chordal progressions. This conflicted with a

8 The invention of this type of cadence was for a long time attributed to Francesco Landini (1325-97), but it has since been found in the works of earlier composers of the Ars Nova.

new interest in textural smoothness and blend, and so led composers to select only those triads and progressions that they found
harmonically satisfactory or which could be transformed by the
introduction of *musica ficta.*

These developments can readily be traced in the music of
Taverner, and they provide valuable means of assessing the chronology of a work. Whilst the harmonic progressions in his early
writing are largely the result of independent part-movement, there
is a strong feeling for tonality in his later settings; and in works
such as the *Meane Mass* and *Te Deum* there are passages that have
a distinct leaning towards a major or minor key. Although his
music was still conceived horizontally, there was an increased
awareness of the vertical sound created by the combination of
the different voices, and of the role played by the bass in providing a foundation for the upper parts. There also appeared to be
a greater concern for the *overall* progression from one chord to
another, and a conscious effort to achieve harmonic as well as
melodic smoothness. This often necessitated the chromatic altera-
tion of notes, and the increased application of *musica ficta* became
one of the important compositional techniques of the period
contributing towards the gradual transition to tonality.

In addition to the harmonic trends which, to quote the Editors
of *Tudor Church Music*, 'rang the death-knell of the whole modal
system',[9] the second quarter of the sixteenth century was also a
time when composers were beginning to recognise the expressive
and dramatic potential inherent in accented dissonance, whose
most important form was the suspension. The discords resulting
from polyphonic decoration were generally of a transitory nature,
often occurring on weak crotchet beats, and rarely lasting sufficiently long to make any impact of their own. The harmonic
tension created by the suspension, however, was much greater
since it normally fell on an accented beat, and was brought into
sharper relief by the customary consonance of its preceding chord
and its resolution. The technique certainly appealed to Taverner
during his later years, for a number of his works, including the
Meane Mass and *Te Deum*, contain many well-placed suspensions.
They appear both at cadences and during the course of a phrase
in so controlled and deliberate a manner as to indicate that the
composer was becoming increasingly aware of their musical
value. Ex. 29 from the *Sanctus* of the *Meane Mass*, for example,
is more than an accident of part-movement.

9 Preface to T.C.M. Vol. I.

Ex.29

glo - ri - a tu - - - a

Most of Taverner's suspensions occur in the upper voices and only occasionally is the dissonance found in the bass. The majority are of the 4-3 or 7-6 variety, though the 9-8 form is used from time to time. Of these the ninth is nearly always major, and there is a preference for the minor seventh. Unlike the short passing dissonances resulting from polyphonic embellishment, his suspensions are generally given sufficient time to make their full impact with the antecedent, the dissonance itself and its resolution being each at least a minim in length. A suspension is never doubled in another voice part, and a resolution is not often anticipated save in the 9-8 progression where it appears in the bass against the dissonant ninth above. Several decorated forms of resolution can be found, especially at cadences, and many involve clichés whose origins lie in the Gothic tradition; but whilst they may be useful in embellishing an otherwise bald progression, they sometimes weaken the suspension by shortening the point of discord. In spite of these technical shortcomings, however, Taverner's recognition of the musical value of accented dissonance is an important feature of his late style, and at the time made a significant contribution towards the growth of Renaissance harmony.

One aspect of sixteenth-century vocal writing that continues to pose problems is underlay: the wedding of text and music. Its history shows it to be a subject to which mediaeval composers paid little attention. It was not common practice in pre-Tudor times to set words so that their meaning was expressed in the music; in fact they were often totally obscured in the fourteenth-century polytextual motets with their simultaneous use of different languages. Furthermore, little effort was made to ensure that musical and verbal stress coincided, so that in performance words sometimes came through in a distorted form. Even with the abandonment of polytextuality in the fifteenth century, English composers (including John Dunstable, the leading figure of the day) still did not regard word-setting as important in any way. After the death of Dunstable in 1453, a certain elementary projection of the text is apparent from time to time in the choral works of Fayrfax and his contemporaries, but it really amounts to little more than an expression of the obvious. For example, such jubilant phrases as 'in gloria Dei patris', 'Osanna' and 'et resurrexit' were generally given full-choir treatment, whilst the more intimate, devotional passages like 'Qui tollis peccata mundi' and 'Et incarnatus est' were scored for a smaller number of voices. Pictorial representations of 'descendit' and 'ascendit in coelum' became regular features in the settings of the Mass, but there appeared to be little further appreciation of word values, and there were still no systematic attempts to make musical and textual stress coincide. It was in this musical climate that Taverner grew up, and it is therefore not surprising to find a similar attitude to word-setting in his early work.

There are a number of initial problems in the study of Renaissance underlay. The first is that different manuscript sources of the same work often vary in the distribution of the text, so that it is difficult to be sure of the composer's original intentions. Secondly, and more problematic, the text is sometimes wholly or partly missing, and in works built upon a cantus firmus the voice part that carries the chant is frequently left wordless or merely with an opening phrase or *incipit*. Thirdly, copyists have at times added to the confusion by placing more emphasis upon the visual aspect of their manuscripts than upon the correct and accurate alignment of words and notes, so that in performance a great deal must have been left on trust to the singers.

All these problems arise in turn when we come to examine the music of Taverner, and a glance at the Appendix alone will show just how many of his works lack a text in their various manuscript sources. Despite these difficulties, however, it is still possible to distinguish a gradual change in his approach to word-setting during the course of his career. As already shown, a bird's-eye view of his musical development can be seen as a progressive textural clarification from the elaborately florid works of his London and Oxford years to the simpler and more syllabic writing of later pieces like the *Meane Mass*, the *Playn Song Mass* and *Te Deum*. Together with this stylistic change, and aided by it, comes an increased feeling for verbal rhythm and a greater awareness of the relative weight and significance of separate words within a phrase or sentence. Such changes are clearly discernible in Taverner's mature works, where musical and textual stress regularly coincide, and important words and syllables are set to longer note-values or treated melismatically. Whether or not this new approach was a conscious effort on the part of the composer or just a by-product of his leaning towards a simpler musical style it is difficult to say, but the result is a closer bond between words and music, and a more direct projection of the text. Although individual words were still not set in a manner expressive of their mood and meaning — that was to be a late Tudor practice — the *fermata* sign ∩ was used from time to time to focus attention upon some key word in the text such as 'Ave' or 'Jesu'.

A feature that separates Taverner's mature works from those of his earlier years is textual repetition. Prior to his time this practice was totally absent from the English scene, although, like so many compositional techniques, it was already well established in the Netherlands School before the end of the fifteenth century. In Taverner's own writing it does not occur with any degree of regularity until quite late in his career, the *Meane Mass, Te Deum* and *O splendor gloriae* providing the best examples of its use. The choice of words for repetition does not appear to be governed by any literary consideration, and more often than not it is the result of imitation or antiphony. In discussing the *Meane Mass,* (pp. 66ff.) reference was made to imitation by pairs of voices, and Ex. 15 (p. 68) shows both the music and the words of the two leading voices repeated by the answering pair.

Before leaving the subject of text distribution and treatment, it would be appropriate to consider the related subject of form. In early sixteenth-century vocal writing, the design of a work was largely determined by the natural and traditional subdivisions of the text. This was particularly so in extended settings like the Mass. The growth of a composition did not depend upon thematic development beyond the extent to which it was used in imitation, and, unlike Renaissance dances, it did not involve the repetition of whole polyphonic sections. Instead, the music was through-composed, and the only links between movements were those created by the employment of parody-techniques and common opening passages.

Despite the lack of formal designs, however, certain traditions were established in the scoring of late fifteenth-century settings of the Mass and of the Canticles; these traditions acted in a structural capacity, and prevented a work becoming shapeless and its musical ideas diffuse. In the Mass, for example, certain sections of the text like 'Qui sedes ad dexteram patris' in the *Gloria*, 'Et resurrexit tertia die' in the *Credo* and 'Dona nobis pacem' in the *Agnus Dei* were always given full choir treatment, while passages such as 'Et incarnatus est' in the *Credo* and the opening of the *Benedictus* were scored for reduced forces. Antiphony was often employed in the *Credo* section beginning 'Deum de Deo, lumen de lumine' so that interest fluctuated between the entries of upper, middle and lower voices, and certain coda passages like 'Et exspecto resurrectionem' were generally set in a cumulative style.

This variety of vocal scoring according to the natural subdivisions of the text can be found in much of Taverner's writing including the three Festal Masses, and, as in the case of his predecessors, it constitutes an important feature in the design of his works. Nevertheless, it is not the only structural means available to him, and an examination of any of his large-scale compositions reveals an acute awareness on his part of the need for balance both within and between movements. In his Masses he followed Tudor practice by making all four movements of a setting roughly equal in length. This often involved a syllabic treatment of several passages in the long texts of the *Gloria* and *Credo*, and the adoption of a more melismatic style in the shorter *Sanctus* and *Agnus Dei*. Furthermore, the individual movements were often built upon 'tutti' and reduced choir sections which complemented and balanced each other with almost mathematical precision. Admittedly it is easy to read far more into the design of a work than the composer ever intended, but the frequency with which internal balance occurs in Taverner's writing seems to rule out the possibility of it being anything other than intentional and the result of careful planning. Works based upon a cantus firmus have a built-in structural aid, and generally speaking it is put to good use. This is apparent at an early stage in the *Western Wind* Mass where the melody occurs without a break throughout the setting and is distributed equally between all four movements. But even in those Masses and Antiphons where there is no supporting cantus firmus, with very few exceptions the structural scheme is always clear and sectional balance is always present. In his later works, when the use of full-choir polyphony throughout a piece began to replace the earlier practice of varying the vocal scoring at each fresh subdivision of the text, Taverner continues to pay close attention to form and design. For example, in his Festal Antiphon *O splendor gloriae*, the main structural device is imitation, which occurs at the beginning of each section of the work and carries the listener naturally from one musical idea to the next. Again, in *Gaude plurimum* and *Quemadmodum*, imitation plays a similar part, and in addition there is a successful attempt to create overall balance by building each piece on a binary plan.

It might perhaps be said that Taverner's contribution to the growth of form and design was less marked than in other directions, especially in the development of melodic and harmonic technique. Nevertheless, it is interesting to observe that, from the very outset of his career, he was keenly aware of the need for structure and balance in a musical work and made a conscious effort to find ways of satisfying those requirements.

CODA

In the final count, where exactly does John Taverner stand in the history of music?

Was he in any way an influential figure? Did he make any notable contribution to the growth and development of music? And do his works rank as outstanding essays of their time? In short, was he a great composer or not?

These questions are easier to ask than to answer, for in Taverner we are dealing with a complex personality who lived and worked during a most unstable period in this country's history, and also at a time when the art of composition was undergoing a major change. Moreover, his work and his appointments were such that he could not fail to be affected by the religious, political and social events of the day.

In his monumental study of Bach,[1] Albert Schweitzer differentiates between the subjective and the objective artist. The former is the pioneer, seeking out and establishing new modes of expression, while the latter accepts existing practices and techniques, and carries them to full fruition. The first heralds a new era; the second sums up the old one. The present study has shown Taverner to be a product of the mediaeval tradition, and the last composer of any consequence to build upon Gothic principles. In this respect he was an objective artist. But equally there are subjective elements in his writing: the increased use of imitation, a leaning towards greater musical and textual clarity and a growing interest in major-minor tonality, all of them characteristic of Renaissance thought. On the one hand, he sums up the principles inherited from Fayrfax and other fifteenth-century composers in a final flowering of mediaeval polyphony. On the other, he is an artist working during a period of transition, whose fertile imagination at times outruns the technical resources of the day.

Despite the forward trends in his writing, however, Taverner cannot be said to have exerted any real influence upon later com-

1 Albert Schweitzer: *J. S. Bach*, trans. Ernest Newman, A. & C. Black, 1923.

posers in this country, and certainly none abroad. Although much of his music has been preserved by such devotees as Edward Paston of Norfolk, there is no evidence to suggest that it was widely used, even in those households that continued to pay allegiance to Rome. A few settings including the *Meane Mass* and *Small Devotion*, and the Antiphons *Gaude plurimum* and *Mater Christi* were perpetuated in versions adapted to English words, but again performances appear to have depended very much upon enthusiasts for the music, much as they have done in our own century. It is therefore difficult to measure Taverner's contribution to the development of music, for a study of his work shows him to have played an important part in the growth of certain compositional processes but at the same time no single technique or innovation can be solely attributed to him.

It is also difficult to say whether or not he was a great composer, for wherein lies greatness? Clearly works like *Gloria tibi Trinitas, O splendor gloriae*, the *Meane Mass* and *Quemadmodum* could all be termed masterpieces, but other settings fall far short of that description. Even the comparisons that some historians have drawn (often to the detriment of Taverner) with the other two T's of sixteenth-century England, Tallis and Tye, fail to provide an accurate picture of our subject. In the first place, the creative life of both composers far exceeded that of Taverner[2]; and secondly, their output extended well beyond the field of sacred Latin polyphony into settings for the Reformed Church, into secular song and instrumental writing.

So what can be said in the final assessment?

Perhaps Taverner's achievements can best be summarised by saying that he helped to effect a smooth transition from mediaeval to Renaissance musical thought by preserving the most worthwhile features of the old style and grafting on to them the first principles of the new art, all within an age fraught with problems of Church and State. In other words, he was an essential link between two great periods of English musical history.

This is not to imply that his role was merely catalytic, however, for he expresses himself in an individual and recognizable voice, and one that continues to attract its followers and supporters. Experience has shown that this personal voice yields up its qualities gradually at each fresh hearing, and the present writer is not alone in finding that repeated participation in Taverner's music leads to ever-increasing enjoyment, satisfaction and respect.

Surely no composer could wish for more.

2 Tallis: c.1505-85; Tye: c.1497-1572.

APPENDIX

A LIST OF THE MANUSCRIPT SOURCES OF TAVERNER'S MUSIC

LONDON: BRITISH MUSEUM

1. *MS. Royal Appendix 56.* A book containing a miscellaneous collection of songs and keyboard music, thought to have been compiled for the Henrician Court during the second decade of the sixteenth century. It includes an excerpt from the opening of the *Agnus Dei* from Taverner's *Western Wind* Mass (treble and tenor voices only) arranged in keyboard format.

2. *MS. Harley 1709.* A meane part-book, being the only surviving one of five, possibly dating from about 1520 and originally belonging to the Chapel Royal. It contains a miscellaneous collection of mainly Marian motets by various Tudor composers including Taverner's *Gaude plurimum* and *Ave Dei patris filia*, both unattributed.

3. *MS. Add. 34191.* A late Henrician bass part-book, possibly one of five, containing Masses and miscellaneous works for both the Sarum Rite and the English Church, amongst which is Taverner's Votive Antiphon *Gaude plurimum.*

4. *MSS. Add. 17802-5.* Four of an original set of five manuscripts — the tenor is missing — known as the 'Gyffard' part-books, possibly dating from the third quarter of the sixteenth century, and containing Masses, various works for the Sarum Rite and a setting of the Passion. These books are important in that they are the sole source of eight of Taverner's compositions, namely the *Playn Song Mass, Kyrie Leroy, Alleluia Salve Virgo*, the four-part *Magnificat, Audivi vocem de caelo, Gloria in excelsis, In pace in idipsum* and the four-part *Dum transisset*. Also included is the earlier version of *Alleluia Veni electa mea* and one of the two complete copies of the *Western Wind* Mass.

5. *MS. Add. 4900.* A copy of the *Catalogue of the Bishops of England* of 1601 with an appendix of music manuscripts, possibly of an earlier date, including an arrangement for solo voice with lute accompaniment of Taverner's *Alleluia Veni electa mea.*

6. *MSS. Add. 18936-9.* Four of an original set of five part-books containing a miscellaneous collection of sacred and secular vocal music, and the sole source of the three three-part settings by Taverner of *Christe eleison.* Also included are excerpts from his six-part *Magnificat,* the sequence verse *Traditur militibus* and *Gaude plurimum,* the last two incorrectly labelled *Benedictus* and *Sanctus* respectively. An *Osanna in excelsis* attributed to Taverner is now regarded as spurious. All the above works are without text.

7. *MS. Add. 29246.* A lute book from the early seventeenth century in which five of the transcriptions are excerpts from Taverner's works, namely the Masses *Corona spinea, Gloria tibi Trinitas* and *Sine Nomine* or *Meane Mass,* the Antiphon *Gaude plurimum* and the Prose *Sospitati dedit aegros.* An excerpt from a Tallis motet is wrongly attributed to Taverner.

8. *MS. Add. 31390.* A book of miscellaneous pieces for voices or instruments in five to eight parts, dating from about 1578 and containing one of the two copies of Taverner's five-part *Dum transisset II,* and one of the three surviving copies of his *Quemadmodum.* Both are without text and unattributed.

9. *MS. Add. 34049.* A treble part-book from the early seventeenth century containing unattributed Marian settings including two Taverner Antiphons, *Gaude plurimum* and *Mater Christi,* and the Prose *Sospitati dedit aegros.*

10. *MSS. Add. 41156-8.* Three of a set of five part-books (treble, meane and countertenor) containing a miscellaneous collection of instrumental pieces including Taverner's *Gaude plurimum* and *Sospitati dedit aegros.* Apart from an introductory phrase or *incipit,* both are without text and both are unattributed.

11. *MS. Royal Music Library 24 d. 2.* An early seventeenth-century commonplace book written by the 'celebrated copyist of Queen Elizabeth's time',[1] John Baldwin, Gentleman of the Chapel Royal, containing a variety of compositions from the years 1581 to 1606. It is an important manuscript in that it is the sole source of four Taverner works, namely the two short three-part Marian Antiphons, *Prudens Virgo* and *Virgo pura,* as well as the sequence verse *Jesu spes poenitentibus* and the Tract verse *Tam peccatum.* In addition there is one of the three extant copies of *Traditur militibus,* and excerpts from *Gaude plurimum* and the Mass *Gloria tibi Trinitas,* the first and third titles without text.

LONDON: ROYAL COLLEGE OF MUSIC

12. *MS. 2035.* A complete set of three part-books dating from the late sixteenth or early seventeenth centuries containing mainly excerpts from a variety of sacred works including Taverner's Masses *Corona spinea, Gloria tibi Trinitas* and *Sine Nomine* or *Meane Mass*, his Antiphons *Ave Dei patris filia* and *Gaude plurimum*, and the Prose *Sospitati dedit aegros*. This manuscript is also the sole source of a separate three-part *Agnus Dei* which is of doubtful authorship. (An excerpt from a Tallis motet is incorrectly attributed to Taverner.)

OXFORD: THE BODLEIAN LIBRARY

13. *MSS. Music School, e. 376-381.* These manuscripts, known as the Forrest-Heyther part-books, are high in order of importance, since they are the only complete source of the three six-part Festal Masses by Taverner. The collection opens with *Gloria tibi Trinitas* which, together with the next ten Masses, was copied by an unknown hand during the time that the composer was at Oxford.[2] In 1530, according to one of the manuscripts (No. 378), the part-books were in the possession of Canon William Forrest of Cardinal College, who added another seven Masses including Taverner's *Corona spinea* and *O Michael*. It is possible that the original eleven Masses were collected, copied and bound expressly for use in Wolsey's Chapel, and that the *Informator* had some part in the compilation of the books since three other composers represented — Aston, Fayrfax and Ashewell — all had associations with Northern England and, in particular, Lincolnshire.

14. *MSS. Music School, e. 420-22.* Three part-books of an original four — the tenor is missing — known as the Wanley Manuscripts, dating from the middle of the sixteenth century and containing ten services for the English Church, including adaptations of the *Meane Mass* and *Sancti Wilhelmi* or *Small Devotion*, and the Antiphon *Mater Christi* set to the words 'God be merciful unto us'.

15. *MSS Music School, e. 1-5.* A set of five part-books dated 1585, originally owned and probably copied by John Sadler, containing mainly Latin Church music including four Taverner Antiphons, *Ave Dei patris filia, Gaude plurimum, Mater Christi* and *O splendor gloriae*, as well as the *Western Wind* Mass.

16. *MS. Music School, e. 423.* A countertenor part-book — the sole surviving one from a set of five — dating from the late sixteenth century, and containing a miscellaneous collection of sacred and secular vocal works as well as some instrumental music. Included are three Taverner Antiphons, *Ave Dei patris filia, Gaude plurimum* and *Mater Christi*, and the six-part *Magnificat*.

OXFORD: CHRIST CHURCH

17. *MS. 45.* A late sixteenth-century book containing mainly two, three and four-part excerpts from various Latin Church works, and including Taverner's *Traditur militibus* and sections of the six-part *Magnificat.*

18. *MSS. 979-83.* An important set of five part-books of an original six — the tenor is missing — dated 1581 and containing Latin Church music and some instrumental works in the hand of John Baldwin, a lay-clerk at St George's Chapel, Windsor. The collection is the sole source of Taverner's Verse *Ecce Mater* and his setting of the *Te Deum.* Also included are the Antiphons *Ave Dei patris filia, Christe Jesu pastor bone, Gaude plurimum, Mater Christi* and *O splendor gloriae*, two five-part settings of *Dum transisset Sabbatum, Quemadmodum* (without text) and the Mass *Gloria tibi Trinitas.* A footnote in the last manuscript (No. 983) reads: 'Mr John Tavernor of Cardinal Wolsey's Chapel who died in Boston and there lieth.'

19. *MSS. 984-88.* A complete set of five part-books mainly copied by Robert Dow from 1581 onwards, containing a miscellaneous collection of sacred and secular vocal works and some instrumental music. This manuscript is the only complete source of Taverner's five-part *Dum transisset Sabbatum I.*

CAMBRIDGE: KING'S COLLEGE

20. *Rowe Music Library, MS. 316.* The sole surviving part-book (meane) of an original five copied about 1580, containing a miscellaneous collection of vocal and instrumental works including Taverner's Antiphons *Gaude plurimum* and *Mater Christi* adapted to the English words 'I will magnify Thee' and 'O most Holy and Mighty Lord' respectively.

CAMBRIDGE: PETERHOUSE

21. *MSS. 40, 41, 31, 32.* The 'Henrician' set of manuscripts comprising four part-books of an original five — the tenor and some pages of the treble are missing — copied sometime before the mid-sixteenth century, and containing no less than twelve works by Taverner. It is a particularly important set since it is the sole surviving source of six of these works, namely the Mass *Mater Christi*, the five-part *Magnificat*, and the Antiphons *Ave Maria, Fac Nobis, Sancte Deus* and *Sub tuum praesidium.* Also included are the *Meane Mass* and *Missa Sancti Wilhelmi* or *Small Devotion*, and the Antiphons *Ave Dei patris filia, Christe Jesu pastor bone, Gaude plurimum* and *Mater Christi.*

22. *MSS. 44, 43, 37, 35.* Four part-books (*decani* meane, tenor and bass, and *cantoris* tenor) from the second set of the Caroline manuscripts dating from around 1635, containing mainly music for the English Church, but including Taverner's *Meane Mass* with its original Latin text.

CAMBRIDGE: ST JOHN'S COLLEGE

23. *MS. K. 31.* A bass part-book from an original set of five or six, dating from about 1520, containing Masses and Marian Motets for use in the Chapel Royal. Taverner is represented by *Ave Dei patris filia* and *Gaude plurimum.*

CAMBRIDGE: UNIVERSITY LIBRARY

24. *MS. Dd. 13. 27.* A countertenor part-book, companion to the above manuscript (K. 31) and from the same original set, again containing the Antiphons *Ave Dei patris filia* and *Gaude plurimum.*

ST MICHAEL'S COLLEGE, TENBURY

25. *MSS. 341-44.* Four part-books from a set of five — the bass is missing — dating from about 1600, containing sacred works to Latin texts including Taverner's Antiphon *Mater Christi* and the Prose *Sospitati dedit aegros.* The second of these manuscripts (No. 342) also contains excerpts from three of his Masses, *Corona spinea, Gloria tibi Trinitas* and *Sancti Wilhelmi* or *Small Devotion*, and from the Votive Antiphon, *Gaude plurimum.*

26. *MSS. 354-58.* A full set of five part-books dating from the early seventeenth century, containing Latin Church settings similar to the above manuscript. Included are Taverner's Antiphons *Gaude plurimum* and *Mater Christi*, and short excerpts from the *Meane Mass, Gloria tibi Trinitas*, the six-part *Magnificat, Ave Dei patris filia* and *Sospitati dedit aegros.*

27. *MSS. 807-811.* Five part-books from a set of six — the treble is missing — dating from the early seventeenth century, containing mainly Latin Church settings including Taverner's six-part *Magnificat.*

28. *MS. 1464.* A bass part-book, the only surviving one of a set of five or so, copied around 1575, containing a miscellaneous collection of sacred and secular vocal works together with some instrumental music. Included are Taverner's *Gloria tibi Trinitas, Sancti Wilhelmi* or *Small Devotion* and the *Meane Mass.*

29. *MSS. 1469-71.* Treble, countertenor and bass part-books from a set of five copied towards the end of the sixteenth century, containing a miscellaneous collection of sacred and secular vocal

works, including Taverner's *Gaude plurimum, Sospitati dedit aegros* and part of the Mass *Gloria tibi Trinitas.* A further work, *Ave Regina,* is incorrectly attributed to him.

30. *MS. 1486.* A tenor part-book, one of two manuscripts from an original set of five, copied by John Sadler in 1591 and containing a collection of motets including Taverner's *Gaude plurimum.* It also contains the wrongly attributed work, *Ave Regina,* referred to above.

WORCESTERSHIRE RECORD OFFICE, WORCESTER

31. *The Willmott MS.* A meane part-book, companion to the above (MS. 1486), containing *Gaude plurimum* and the incorrectly attributed motet, *Ave Regina.*

ESSEX RECORD OFFICE, CHELMSFORD

32. *MS. D/DP. Z. b/1.* A bass part-book dating from about 1590, containing mainly sacred settings, including six works of Taverner, namely the *Meane Mass,* the Antiphons *Gaude plurimum, Mater Christi* and *O splendor gloriae,* and *Quemadmodum* and *Sospitati dedit aegros,* the last two without text.

LONDON: BRITISH MUSEUM

33a. *MS. K.1.e.1.* The bass part-book from a set of four, printed in London in 1530 under the title *XX Songes.* It contains secular vocal polyphony by a group of composers, several of whom were associated with the early Tudor Court. Included are four songs by Taverner: *In women is rest peas and pacience, Love wyll I and leve, Mi hart my mynde,* and *The bella, the bella.*

LONDON: WESTMINSTER ABBEY LIBRARY

33b. Three fragments of the treble and meane part-books belonging to the above set of four.

N.B. The many sixteenth- and seventeenth-century manuscript sources containing the *In Nomine* from the *Benedictus* of Taverner's Mass *Gloria tibi Trinitas* have not been included in the above list.

NOTES:

1 According to Charles Burney.

2 J. D. Bergsagel: 'The Date and Provenance of the Forrest-Heyther Collection of Tudor Masses', *Music and Letters,* XLIV, 1963, p. 240.

SELECT BIBLIOGRAPHY

BOOKS, ARTICLES AND ARCHIVE MATERIAL

Baillie, Hugh. 'A London Church in Early Tudor Times', *Music and Letters*, XXXVI, 1955, pp. 55-64.
'A London Gild of Musicians, 1460-1530', *Proceedings of the Royal Musical Association*, LXXXIII, 1956-7, pp. 15-28.
'Squares', *Acta Musicologica*, XXXII, 1960, pp. 178-93.

Bergsagel, John. 'The Date and Provenance of the Forrest-Heyther Collection of Tudor Masses', *Music and Letters*, XLIV, 1963, pp. 240-48.

Boston Town Hall, Lincolnshire. *Borough of Boston Council Minutes*, Vol. I, June 1545-May 1607.

Bray, Roger. 'The Gyffard Part-Books: An Index and Commentary', *The Royal Musical Association Research Chronicle*, VII, 1969, pp. 31-50.

Brett, Philip. 'Edward Paston (1550-1630): A Norfolk Gentleman and his Musical Collection', *Transactions of the Cambridge Bibliographical Society*, Vol. IV, Part I, 1964, pp. 51-69.

Brewer, J. S., Gairdner, J. & Brodie, R. H. (Eds.) *Letters and Papers, Foreign and Domestic, of the Reign of Henry VIII*, H. M. Stationery Office, London.

Burney, Charles. *A General History of Music*, Ed. Frank Mercer, Dover, 1957.

Caldwell, John. *English Keyboard Music before the Nineteenth Century*, Blackwell (Oxford), 1973.

Caley, J. & Hunter, J. (Eds.) *Valor Ecclesiasticus*, London Record Commission, 1810-34.

Clark, Andrew. *The Colleges of Oxford*, Methuen, 1891.

Collins, H. B. 'John Taverner' (Part II), *Music and Letters*, VI, 1925, pp. 314-29.
'John Taverner's Masses', *Music and Letters*, V, 1924, pp. 322-34.

Davison, Nigel. 'The Western Wind Masses', *Musical Quarterly*, LVII, 1971, pp. 427-43.

Davy, Henry. *History of English Music*, J. Curwen, 1895.
'John Taverner', *Dictionary of National Biography*, Vol. XIX, Oxford University Press, 1917.

Doe, Paul. 'Latin Polyphony under Henry VIII', *Proceedings of The Royal Musical Association*, CXV, 1968-9, pp. 81-96.

Donington, Robert & Dart, Thurston. 'The Origin of the In Nomine', *Music and Letters*, XXX, 1949, pp. 101-6.

Elton, G. R. *England under the Tudors*, Methuen, 1955.

Fellowes, E. H. 'John Taverner', *Grove's Dictionary of Music and Musicians*, 5th Edn. 1954, Vol. VIII, pp. 323-4.

Flood, W. H. Grattan. 'New Light on Early Tudor Composers, XII — John Taverner', *Musical Times*, LXI, 1920, pp. 597-8.

Foster, C. W. (Ed.) *Administrations in the Consistory Court, Lincoln*, Lincoln Record Society, 1921.
Calendars of Lincoln Wills, 1320-1600, British Record Society, 1902.

Foxe, John. *Acts and Monuments*, 1563 & 1583 Edns., London Company of Stationers.

Frere, W. H. (Ed.) *Antiphonale Sarisburiense*, Plainsong and Medieval Music Society, 1901-26.
The Use of Sarum, Gregg (reprint), 1969.

Hannas, Ruth. 'Concerning Deletions in the Polyphonic Mass Credo', *Journal of the American Musicological Society*, Vol. V, 1952, pp. 155-86.

Harrison, Frank Ll. *Music in Medieval Britain*, Routledge & Kegan Paul, 1963.
(Ed.) *The Eton Choirbook, Musica Britannica*, Vols. X, XI & XII, Stainer & Bell, 1962.

Harvey, John. 'The Building Works and Architects of Cardinal Wolsey', *Journal of the British Archaelogical Association*, Vol. VIII, 1943, pp. 50-59.

Hawkins, John. *General History of the Science and Practice of Music*, reprints Novello, 1853 and Dover, 1963.

Henderson, W. G. (Ed.) *Processionale Sarum*, Gregg (reprint), 1969.

Hughes, Dom A. & Abraham, G. (Eds.) *New Oxford History of Music*, Vol. III, Oxford University Press, 1960.

le Huray, Peter. *Music and the Reformation in England*, Herbert Jenkins, 1967.

Josephson, David. 'John Taverner: An English Renaissance Master', *American Choral Review*, Vol. IX (2), 1967, pp. 6-15.
'The Festal Masses of John Taverner', *American Choral Review*, Vol. IX (3), 1967, pp. 10-21.
'John Taverner: Smaller Liturgical Works', *American Choral Review*, Vol. IX (4), 1967, pp. 26-41.

Parker, J. H. *Statutes of the Colleges of Oxford*, H. M. Commissioners, Oxford, 1853.

Proctor, F. & Wordsworth, C. (Eds.) *Breviarum ad Usum Sarum*, Cambridge University Press, 1879-86.

Reese, Gustave. *Music in the Renaissance*, Norton, 1959.
'The Origins of the English In Nomine', *Journal of the American Musicological Society*, Vol. II, 1949, pp. 7-22.

Robbins, R. H. (Ed.) *Secular Lyrics of the XIVth and XVth Centuries*, Oxford Press, 1956.

Rogers, Alan. *A History of Lincolnshire*, Darwen Finlayson, 1970.

Simpson, Wm. D. (Ed.) *The Building Accounts of Tattershall College*, Lincoln Record Society, Vol. LV, 1960.

Smith, R. B. *Land and Politics in the England of Henry VIII*, Oxford Press, 1970.

State Papers of King Henry VIII (in 11 volumes), H. M. Stationery Office, 1830-52.

Stevens, Denis. 'John Taverner', *Die Musik in Geschichte und Gegenwart*, Vol. XIII, cols. 152-6, Bärenreiter, 1949-68.
Tudor Church Music, Faber & Faber, 1966.

Stevens, John. *Music and Poetry in the Early Tudor Court*, Methuen, 1961.
(Ed.) *Music at the Court of Henry VIII*, *Musica Britannica*, Vol. XVIII, Stainer & Bell, 1962.

Thompson, Alex. H. *Tattershall: The Manor, the Castle, the Church*, Huddock, 1928.
(Ed.) *Visitations in the Diocese of Lincoln, 1517-31*, Vols. XXXIII, XXXV & XXXVII, Lincoln Record Society, 1940-47.

Thompson, Pishey. *The History and Antiquities of Boston*, J. Noble (Boston), 1856.

Tipping, H. A. *Tattershall Castle, Lincolnshire*, Jonathan Cape, 1929.

INDEX

Alcock, Bishop   16
Alternatim performance   72f., 84, 86, 88f. 90f
Alvard, Thomas   27
Antiphony   43, 64, 66, 67, 98, 102, 110
Appulby, Thomas   16
Aragon, Catherine of   27
Ashwell, Thomas   95n
Aston, Hugh   18, 21n., 39
Augustinians   32

Baldwin, John   76, 81, 83, 84, 88, 91, 92
Beaufort, Margaret   13, 16
Benbow, John   27
Benham, Hugh   19, 69
Billingborough   15
Boston   14, 19, 24, 28f
   Borough of   31
   Parish Church   29, 30, 34, 35
Brett, Philip   82
Buck, P.C.   10
Burney, Charles   9, 10
Byrton, Thomas   26

Cadences   105
Caldwell, John   51
Cambridge   21, 24
Canon   50, 54f., 63, 74, 98f., 104
Cantus firmus use & technique:
   plainsong   40, 41, 42, 47, 51, 52, 72, 77, 84, 86f., 91, 103, 108
   secular   55f
Cardinal College, Oxford:
   building of   20
   post of choirmaster   22
   refounding by Henry VIII   27
   services   23, 80
   staff   21
   statutes   21, 23
Carmelites   32
Carol   95
Caxton, William   16
Chapel Royal   17, 18